MANUFACTURING SUCCESS IN GEORGIA

An Illustrated History

by Jason Moss and Dianne Dent Wilcox

*A publication of the
Georgia Manufacturing Alliance*

First Edition

Copyright 2021 Georgia Manufacturing Alliance

All rights reserved. No part of this book may be reproduced in any form or by any means, electronic or mechanical, including photocopying, without permission in writing from the publisher. All inquiries should be addressed to Georgia Manufacturing Alliance, 930 New Hope 11-102, Lawrenceville, Georgia 30045. Phone 770-338-0051.

www.georgiamanufacturingalliance.com

Rights to the images in this book, except for those in the public domain, are the property of the individuals or organizations that provided them; these images may not be reproduced in any form without consent of the right holders.

IABN: 978-0-9976338-8-7

Manufacturing Success in Georgia – An Illustrated History

author:	Jason Moss
contributing author:	Dianne Dent Wilcox
editor:	Cokkie Eaker
production:	Carol Eyler

CONTENTS

IV	DEDICATION	
V	PREFACE	
VI	INTRODUCTION	
1	Chapter 1	Early Georgia Trading: James Oglethorpe, Tomochichi, and Mary Muskgrove
8	Chapter 2	Georgia Heritage, Diversity, and Manufacturing: Bona Allen Tannery in Buford
20	Chapter 3	Cotton is King: Textile Manufacturing, The Cotton Gin, and The Battlefield: Jefferson Mills, Lummus, Tift Mills and the Young Children, Standard Textile, Bibb Manufacturing, Jarrell Plantation and Griswoldville
30	Chapter 4	Textiles, Carpet, and Flooring: Shaw Industries, World Carpets, Beaulieu of America, Interface, Inc., J & J Industries, and Carpet Capital of the World
37	Chapter 5	Major Changes in the Nineteenth Century: Railroad Expansion, Ammunition and Firearms, Shoes, Civil War Textiles, Total War and an Emerging New South
46	Chapter 6	Food Industries: Cola, Pecans, Peanuts, Onions, Chickens: Pilgrim's Pride, Fieldale Farms, Crider Foods, Cagle's, Chick-fil-A, and Colas
57	Chapter 7	The Transportation Industry: Georgia Ports Authority, Brunswick Auto Port, Ford, GM, KIA, Blue Bird, E-Z Go, Club Car, and Great Dane
69	Chapter 8	Early Timber Harvesting and Wood Products: The Dodge Company, Lumber Mills, Pinola, Inc., Charles Herty, Henry Tift, Jim L. Gillis, Jr., International Paper, Graphic Packaging, Pratt, Georgia Pacific, and WestRock
84	Chapter 9	Aviation: Hartsfield-Jackson Atlanta International Airport, Charles Lindberg, Ben Epps, Maule Air, Thrush Aircraft, Lockheed Martin, Gulfstream, Delta, Eastern, The Museum of Aviation, The Entomopter, and Spaceport Camden
94	Chapter 10	What the Future Holds: High-Speed Broadband for Everyone: GALILEO, Hargray-ComSouth, Viasat, Southwire, Nanotechnology, Georgia's Technology Corridors, Technology on a Georgia Air Force Base, Georgia Tech, and SoftWear
104	CHAPTER 11	COVID-19
108	CHAPTER 12	Sign-Off
109		SHARING THE HERITAGE
136		WORKS CITED

Dedication

Manufacturing Success in Georgia is dedicated to the memory of Charles Cada Post (1952-2019), whose tireless encouragement helped fuel this project to preserve a part of Georgia's manufacturing history. As the initial co-author, he helped lay out the structure of the book and provided some of the foundational research. Charlie Post was a founding member of the Georgia Manufacturing Alliance (GMA), formerly known as Networking MFG, and President of TSI Solutions in Stone Mountain, Georgia. In the early days of GMA, he coordinated speakers for monthly meetings and challenged those around him to do their very best, with everything they touched. Although Charlie isn't here to see this book's completion, it would not be the same without his contribution.

And also:
Cokkie Eaker, Editor
Kandy Moss
Wesley Moss
Carol Counter

PREFACE

The journey which became Manufacturing Success in Georgia began in 1975 when I was in the first grade. My class at McDonough Primary School took a field trip to the Ford factory in Hapeville, Georgia. I was fascinated with the sights, sounds, and smells of manufacturing. The entire trip was a sensory overload for a six-year-old boy. During this factory tour, we watched as the workers rolled in steel, and rolled out cars. Seeing these workers complete their tasks in perfect harmony was like watching a finely tuned machine operate.

Fortunately, I have been able to spend a good portion of my life helping to support and grow Georgia's manufacturing community through the Georgia Manufacturing Alliance (GMA), an organization I founded in 2008. The goal for GMA is to provide opportunities for industry experts to see world class manufacturing process in action through factory tours. As a bonus, we help leaders make valuable connections, so that they can support each other's successes.

I'm thankful for the hundreds of factories that have welcomed us in to visit their operation. I still feel like that little six-year-old boy on my first tour. The machines are often mesmerizing, but the people are the most important part. I love to hang around really smart people, so I can see how they find the perfect solutions to tough problems. The people are the heartbeat of manufacturing, and I want to thank each one who has added to Georgia's rich manufacturing history. This book is about celebrating all of the amazing men and women throughout history who have played a part in Manufacturing Success in Georgia.

Jason Moss
Founder and CEO of the Georgia Manufacturing Alliance

INTRODUCTION

Georgia is one of America's great hubs for manufacturing success. The state has 9,600 manufacturing facilities, which employ nearly 440,000 Georgians. Manufacturing generates almost ten percent of the state's economy, and there is a powerful story behind Georiga's booming manufacturing industry.

Manufacturing has been a part of Georgia's history since its early days, when settlers began farming the rich Georgia soil. Timber and its byproducts led the way with cotton, as the start of a booming agricultural economy. The invention of the cotton gin by Eli Whitney made the boom even bigger.

Manufacturing Success in Georgia tells the amazing story of how a manufacturing segment, rooted in agriculture, has evolved and touched every industry.

Georgia's governors and legislators have been great promoters of manufacturing, as shown by Georgia being the number one state to do business from 2011-2020. A strong manufacturing workforce is also bolstered by the manufacturing curriculum at Georgia Tech, the University of Georgia, and at the twenty-two technical colleges located across the state. Georgia's natural assets make it the ideal location for a manufacturing hub. It is on the eastern seaboard of North America where the original thirteen colonies of the United States first established businesses and travel routes. Georgia's location, then, led to the development of the world's busiest airport, the need for rail accessibility, the building of interstate highways that link Georgia to 80% of the United States population in two days or less, and the Port of Savannah, which is the largest single container terminal in North America and a major link between Georgia and the world.

Manufacturing Success in Georgia looks at what Georgia manufactures, such as leather goods, textiles, cotton gins, soft drinks, chicken products, pecan products, peanut products, automobiles, school buses, golf carts, semi-trailers, pulp and paper, naval stores, aerospace components, aircraft, software, satellites, and more. It looks at progress from a historical perspective, knowing that what Georgia produces now is tomorrow's history.

Finally, *Manufacturing Success in Georgia* looks at the entire state, both urban and rural, and her amazing journey of productivity from using things supplied by nature to crafting nanotechnology tools for the exploration of our world, and beyond.

But the people of Georgia are her biggest manufacturing asset. Living in the heart of the Bible Belt, Georgians combine a strong work ethic with creative ingenuity, and a welcoming spirit. This creates a robust manufacturing community. *Manufacturing Success in Georgia* captures these facts, and more. Our journey has just begun.

Jason Moss
Founder and CEO of the Georgia Manufacturing Alliance
and
Dianne Dent Wilcox
Co-Author

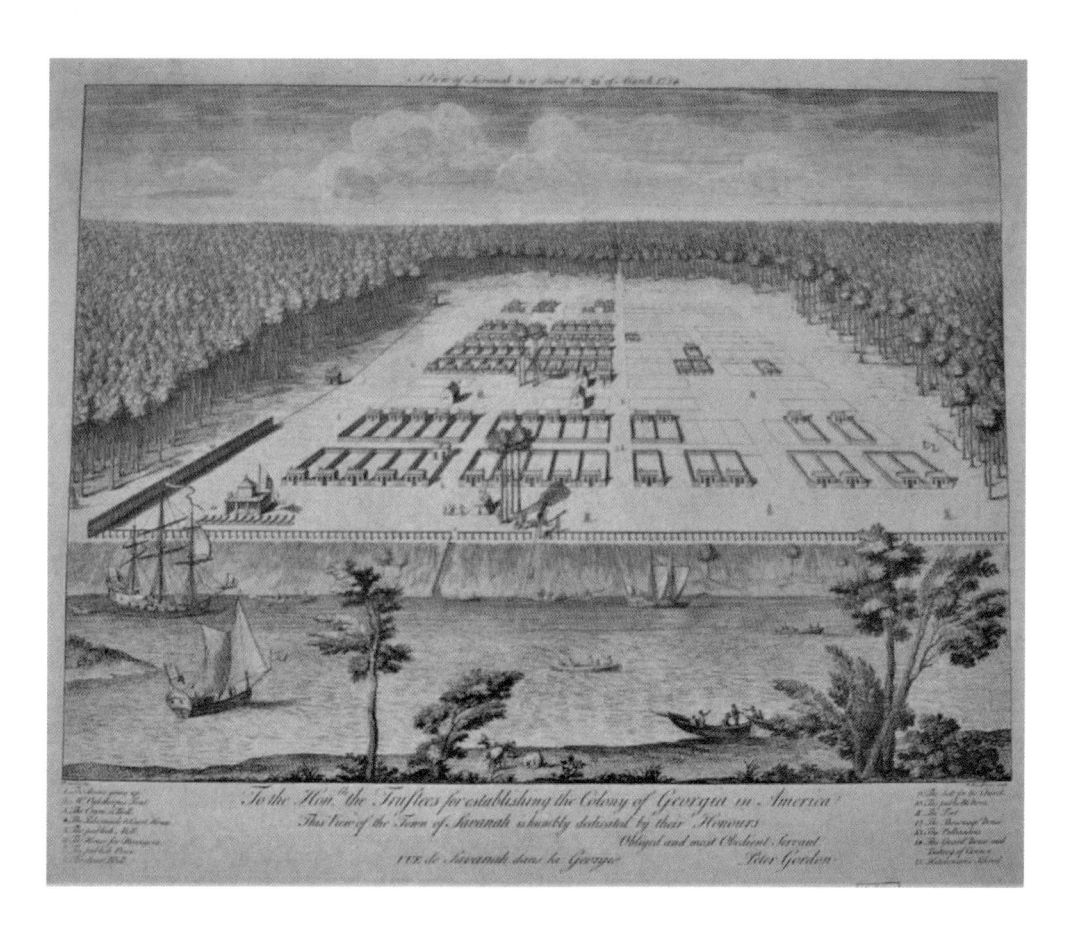

CHAPTER 1

EARLY GEORGIA TRADING

James Oglethorpe, Tomochichi, and Mary Muskgrove

Traders knew Georgia before it was Georgia. Most histories begin with permanent settlements, but the industrious nature of explorers and traders begins our history of *Manufacturing Success in Georgia*. These early traders, investors, and inventors include those indigenous peoples who roamed Georgia as nomads approximately twelve thousand years ago, and the explorers who followed in their footsteps in or before the 1400s. Transportation of goods comes in early, too. Ancient trading paths crisscrossed over what is now the largest state east of the Mississippi as soon as indigenous peoples arrived, according to their legends, from the west. European traders, who had already hunted and fished the New World for a century or more, established small fortified stations for industry and marketing in the 1600s. They brought metal cookware, rifles, beads, and other trade goods to exchange with the locals for corn, skins, squash, venison, and wilderness survival skills. Georgia produced enough trading and resource interest that both

England and Spain wanted colonies on the southwestern frontier of the growing British colonial claims. Although the area seemed uninhabited, people came and went, and the Natives watched.

Edward Teach (c. 1680 – 1718) roamed the waters, islands, rivers, and coasts of South Carolina, Georgia, Florida, and the West Indies, as Blackbeard the Pirate. The British, who had already established colonies north of Georgia, knew that to stay safe, they needed a southern buffer zone. When King George II (1683-1760) authorized James Oglethorpe (1696–1785) to negotiate with the natives and establish a military foothold south of Charleston, South Carolina, Britain claimed the area now known as Georgia, and Oglethorpe successfully established

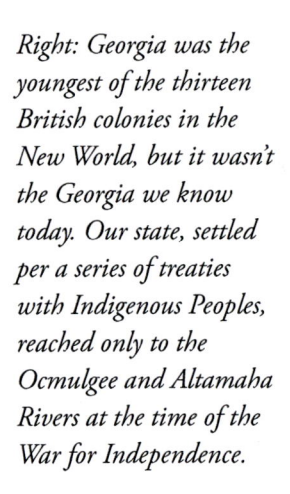

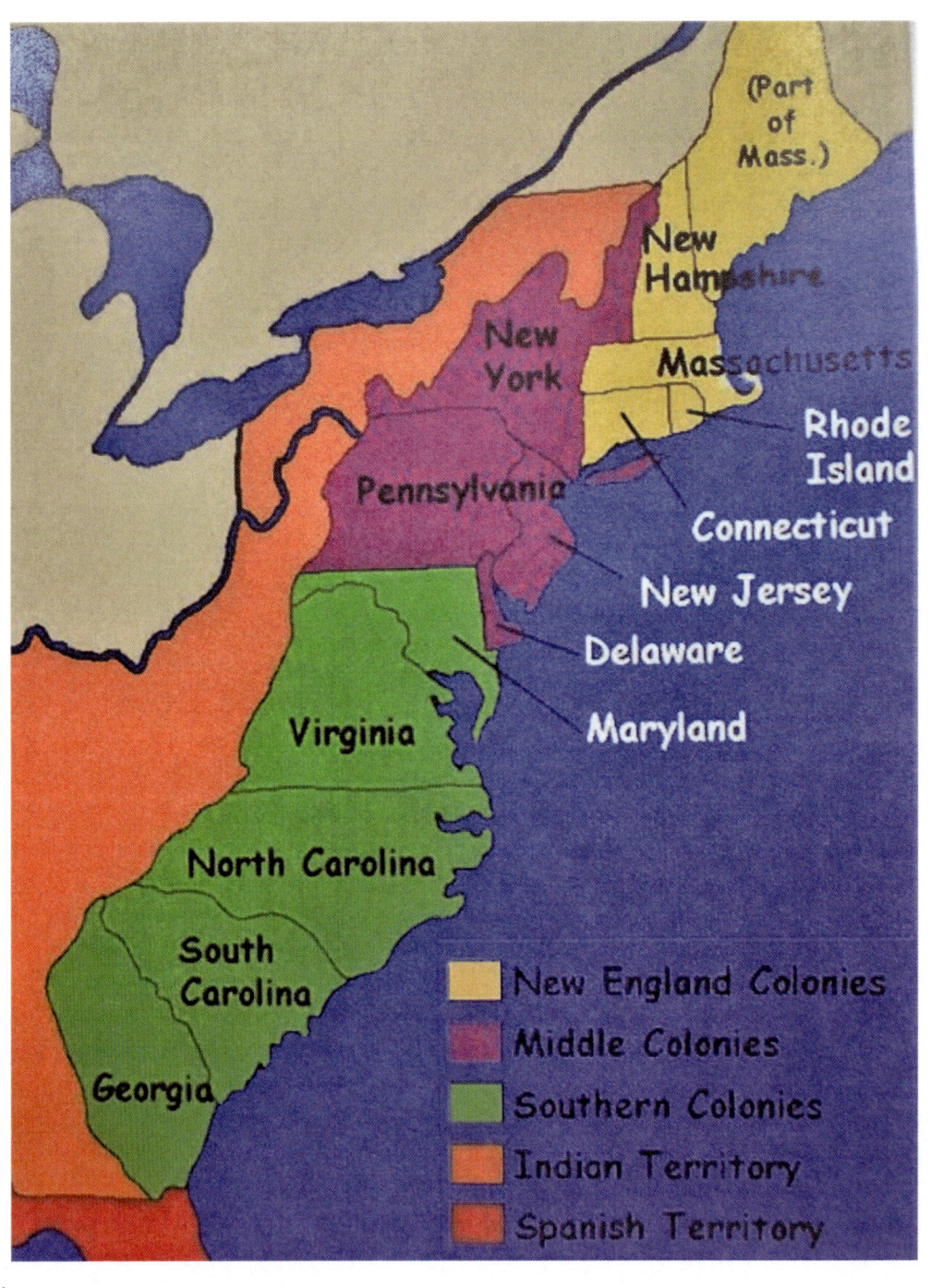

Right: Georgia was the youngest of the thirteen British colonies in the New World, but it wasn't the Georgia we know today. Our state, settled per a series of treaties with Indigenous Peoples, reached only to the Ocmulgee and Altamaha Rivers at the time of the War for Independence.

Manufacturing Success in Georgia

a British/Spanish boundary at the Battle of Bloody Marsh on Saint Simons Island during the War of Jenkins Ear, in 1742. Frederica on Saint Simons with Darien and Savannah on the mainland became centers of trade, industry, investment, invention, crafting, and then manufacturing.

The Georgia colony reached east and west from the Atlantic Ocean to the Ocmulgee River, which joins the Altamaha and goes into the ocean at Darien. The colony reached north and south from the Savannah River to the St. Mary's River. Georgia, then, was the southwestern boundary of the United States, until Tennessee (1796) and Alabama (1819) joined the Union. Florida was admitted to the Union later in 1845.

JAMES OGLETHORPE

Oglethorpe's original interest in establishing Georgia was as a social solution to help what he called "the worthy poor", but the idea quickly gave way to the need for Georgia as a military buffer between England and Spain in the New World. Economic considerations meant that the people chosen for the Georgia colony were skilled workers, self-motivated, and industrious.

No one jailed for debts in England was in the original group of Georgia settlers. This meant that those chosen were both skilled and business savvy: "Although charity had been the initial motivation for the Georgia movement, by 1732, military and economic considerations were the principal factors. As a result of Oglethorpe's persuasive arguments, King George II in 1732 granted a charter for creating Georgia and named Oglethorpe as one of the twenty-one Trustees to govern the new colony. As the Trustees began interviewing potential colonists, they looked for carpenters, tailors, bankers, farmers, merchants, and others with the skills necessary for the colony's success. By this time, any ideas of Georgia being a haven for debtors in English prisons had long vanished – and not one formerly jailed debtor was among the first colonists selected. Georgia's founders thought that the colony's climate would be suitable for the production of valuable silk, wine, and other Mediterranean-type commodities." (Jackson)

Next, the British recruited Scottish soldiers to help settle and defend the new colony: "In 1721, Colonel John Barnwell (1671–1724) began construction of Fort King George near Darien. In 1733, Oglethorpe settled Savannah, and built Fort Frederica. He built Fort St. Simons on St. Simons Island three years later. Scottish Highlanders, mostly from the McIntosh clan, were offered the same opportunity as the English, and many accepted. The Scottish settled in the town of Darien at the mouth of the Altamaha River. A few large plantations were established to grow cotton, indigo, and rice. Many of the citizens hunted and trapped the abundant wild game (deer, wild turkey, and furbearers) in the area." (National Oceanic and Atmospheric Administration Office of Ocean and Coastal Resource Management [OAA] and Georgia Department of Natural Resources Coastal Resources Division)

TOMOCHICHI

British born James Oglethorpe's first treaties in the New World were with Tomochichi (ca. 1644-1739), an indigenous chief who started his own tribe, the Yamacraw, specifically to trade with the English. So involved was Tomochichi in trade, that "In April 1734, Tomochichi, set sail for England with several of his family members and fellow tribesmen to bring requests for education and fair trade directly to the attention of the king and the Trustees of the colony of Georgia. The natives embarked for home at the end of October, after months of conferences and tours, with the sincere belief that their appeals met with a positive reception. During the visit, Tomochichi demonstrated his diplomatic abilities in both political and cultural matters. He acted with respect and restraint, but he remained steadfast in his determination to have his concerns addressed. The maintenance of this delicate balance illustrates his proficiency as a negotiator interested in protecting his people from intrusion and abuse by the Englishmen, but also as an involved beneficiary concerned about the welfare of the new colony." (Sweet)

MARY MUSGROVE

Tomochichi's and Oglethorpe's interpreter was Mary Musgrove (ca. 1700 – ca. 1763). Mary, known to her people as Coosaponakeesa, was the daughter of a Muskogean niece of Emperor Brim and an English trader, Edward Griffin: "She served as a cultural liaison between colonial Georgia and her Native American community in the mid-eighteenth century. Musgrove took advantage of her biculturalism to advocate for Creek interest

Right: An early drawing of Mary Musgrove

Left: The Conner Cabin (1799) at Brewton Parker College in Montgomery County and the Appling County farmhouse (ca. 1870-1900) are Georgia plantation homes.

during treaty negotiations, such as rights to land usage, and payment for services. These negotiations helped maintain peace on the frontier, and expanded Mary's business as a trader. As Pocahontas was to the Jamestown colony and Sacagawea to the Lewis and Clark expedition, so was Musgrove to the burgeoning Georgia colony." (Frank)

When European traders and settlers first came to Georgia, they encountered two major groups of indigenous peoples. The Creek Nation, who called themselves Muskogee, occupied lands of central and South Georgia. The Cherokee occupied north Georgia, and lands in the North and South Carolina colonies. Englishmen called the Muskogee people "Creek"

CHAPTER 1

5

because they found them living near small streams, often called creeks.

Mary/Coosaponakeesa, first married the son of another Creek woman and another English trader, John Musgrove. They worked for the colony as a team. After Musgrove died, Mary married a former indentured servant from her trading post named Jacob Matthews; and after Matthews died, Mary married the controversial minister and trader, Thomas Bosomworth. A leader in her own right, she assisted in the establishment of Georgia with Tomochichi and Oglethorpe by interpreting and actively negotiating: "For over a quarter of a century, colonial Georgia was served by a remarkable, albeit forgotten leader. Mary Musgrove Matthews Bosomworth was a Creek woman of mixed ancestry who consistently provided translation and diplomatic services to James Oglethorpe and other colony leaders during the early years of England's thirteenth colony in North America. Initially, those colonial leaders demonstrated a high level of respect for Mary Musgrove. However, when she began to press for payment for her efforts, they quickly devalued both the woman and her services. Perhaps the cruelest slight has been the continued devaluation of this female leader's place in Georgia's history.

Mary Musgrove "continued to bridge the gap between the two cultures. She continued to act as a liaison between the Creeks and the Europeans for the rest of her life. Salzburger pastors Johann Martin Bolzius and Israel Christian Gronau approached her about instruction in native dialect. John Wesley, the famed Methodist minister, and a Mr. Ingham likewise asked Mary to instruct them. Ingham offered to teach her children to read English in addition to paying for her language services. When Oglethorpe held his meetings with the Creeks and Chickasaws in the summer of 1736, Mary Musgrove was his voice." (Morris)

When Oglethorpe left Georgia, Mary Musgrove Matthews Bosomworth, at one time the wealthiest woman in the colony, continued to assist Major William Horton and Colony President William Stephens, Oglethorpe's successors. It's interesting to note that Georgia's early trading posts were called factories, so even our history foreshadows *Manufacturing Success in Georgia*.

So, trade and the military led the way to establish Georgia as a safe place for industry and manufacturing. Primary military installations were at Darien, Savannah, and on the Sea Islands. Mary Musgrove Matthews Bosomworth received St. Catherine's Island as partial payment for her services to the colony, but in administering this payment, the English relied upon her services once more. Her status in the Muscogee nation kept the southern boundary safe from both Native and Spanish attacks.

Colonial (1600-1775) agricultural ventures in Georgia were in indigo, rice, and sugar. The plantations grew rice and indigo and experimented with citrus and other crops. Settlers began growing cotton near Savannah in 1734, but it did not develop into a lucrative endeavor until 1793, when the cotton gin was invented. Early cotton had short fibers and moving

Manufacturing Success in Georgia

it from the plant to weave it into cloth was labor-intensive. The cultivation of long fiber cotton, named Sea Island for the area in which it was first grown extensively, and mechanization made cotton crops profitable in the 1800s. The word *plantation* means farm. These plantations or farms could be any size. Colonial plantations had plain style homes. In the mid-1800s, farmers began adding Greek Revival features to these older homes to show their success and prominence in the community. When Georgian author Margaret Mitchell's novel *Gone with the Wind* was produced as a feature film in 1939, it featured two Greek Revival mansions as plantation homes. The image of plain style plantation homes seemed to fade as the movie mansion images gained popularity.

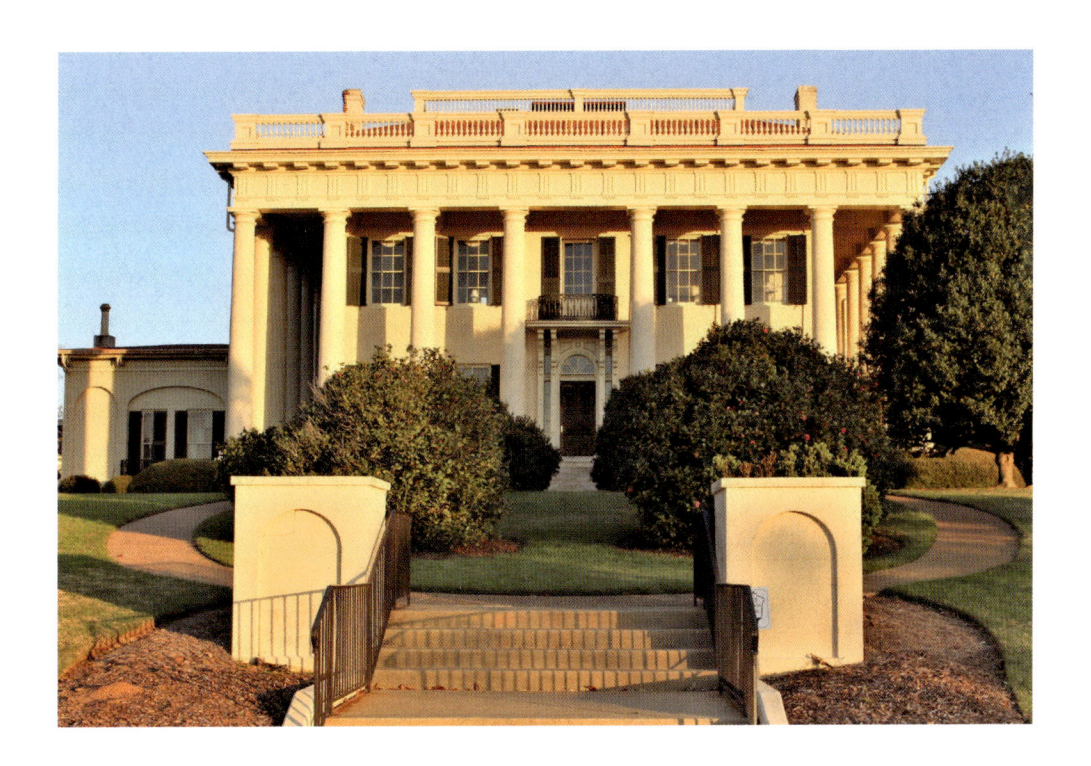

Above: Joseph Bond (1815-1859) lived in this home in Macon. Its Greek Revival style is what most people believe southern plantation homes were like. He set a world record by selling 2,200 bales of cotton for $100,000 in 1857. Bond chose this home, designed by noted architect Elam Alexander for his brother-in-law Jerry Cowles on his community's highest hill, and a grand architectural style for his home to show his success. In 1859, Joseph Bond was killed by a former overseer who he had fired for mistreating a slave. Ironically, the murder occurred at Cowles' new home on College Street. Bond's farm was on property that today is the campus of Wesleyan College. Founded in 1836, with the first buildings on Bond's former plantation in 1928, Wesleyan was the first college in the world chartered to grant degrees to women. Bond's 1836 structure is called the Cowles-Bond-Woodruff House. Cowles, Bond, and Coleman are names of families who lived in the home. Because the house was purchased by the Robert W. Woodruff Foundation, Woodruff is now part of the name. The Woodruff Foundation bought, restored, and gifted the historic mansion to Mercer University. The foundation is "an independent private foundation that seeks to improve the quality of life in Georgia by investing in health, education, economic opportunity, and community vitality." (Robert W. Woodruff Foundation) Woodruff was president of Coca-Cola from 1923 until 1954.

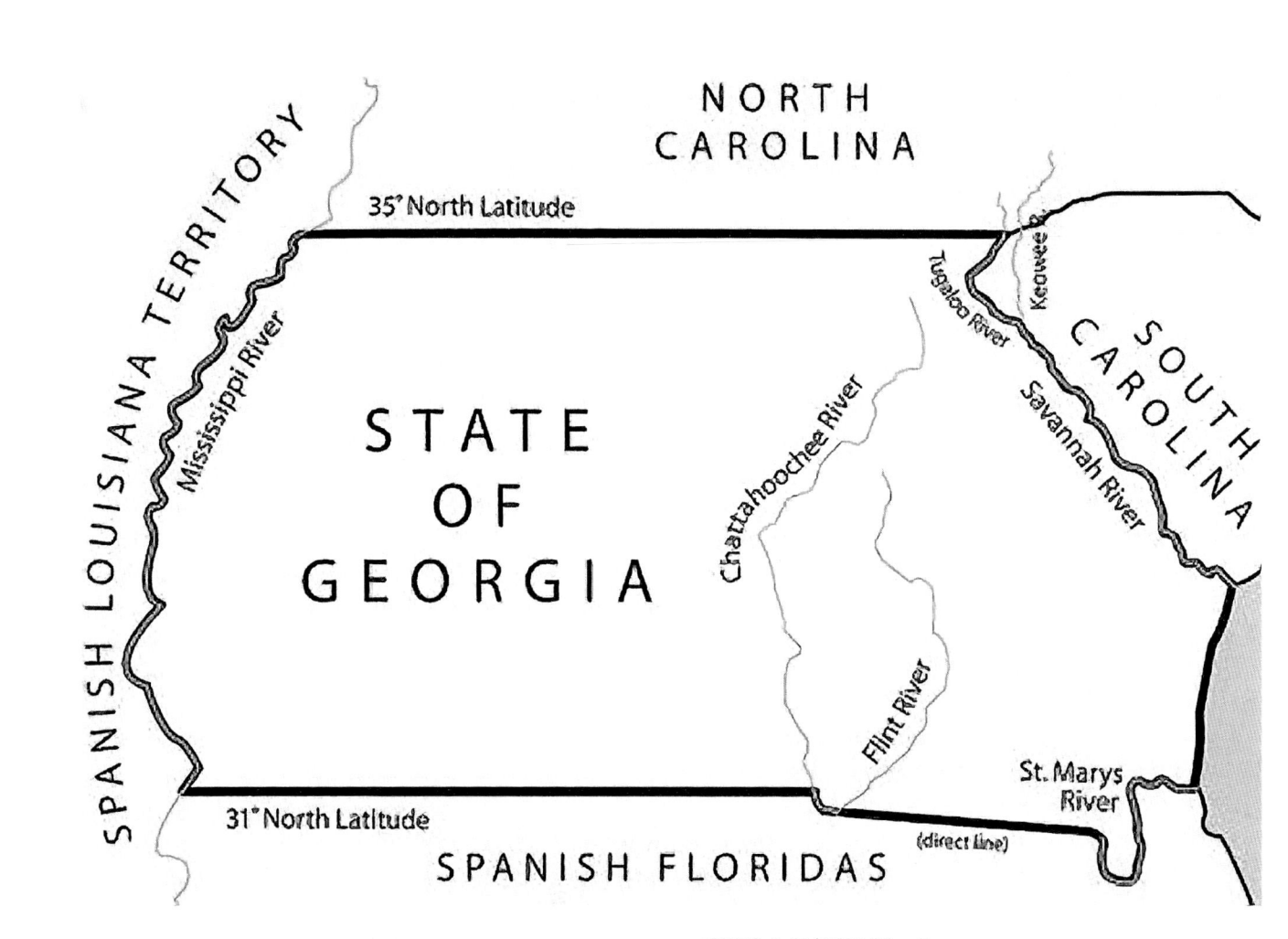

CHAPTER 2

GEORGIA HERITAGE, DIVERSITY, AND MANUFACTURING:

Bona Allen Tannery in Buford

Manufacturing Success in Georgia begins globally in the 1700s with New World colonies providing England with raw materials. Arnold Toynbee (1852–1883), an English economic historian, used the term *Industrial Revolution* to describe England›s economic development from 1760 to 1840. England then held to an economic theory called *Mercantilism* which used colonies as a base for wealth. A one-sided economic system, Mercantilism took the raw material wealth of the colonies and returned only high-priced manufactured goods. Economists cite this as an underlying cause for revolution. Manufacturing, therefore, is the making of new objects from raw materials in mass quantity and using machinery. Mercantilism prompted New World colonists to manufacture their goods. We can argue, then, that social diversity, personal freedom, industry, thrift, and manufacturing success are the basic building blocks on which Georgia and the United States were built.

In Georgia, "Before 1800, the major products of the trade were raw gum (hardened pine tree sap), pitch, and tar. After the American Revolution (1775-1783), processes were developed for distilling spirits of turpentine from gum." (Sullivan)

Raw materials distilled into a new product served as a starting point for manufacturing: "In the late nineteenth and early twentieth centuries, Georgia was the world's leading producer of naval stores, which are materials extracted from southern pine forests and then used in the construction and repair of sailing vessels. Typical naval stores include lumber, railroad ties, rosin, and turpentine" (Sullivan).

Separation from England after the American War for Independence meant the loss of the Royal British Navy for protection, which meant the need for a United States Naval force was essential. England accelerated the need. When the colonies reorganized themselves as independent states, England notified the Barbary Pirates that ships from the New World were unprotected. This prompted the North African states of Morocco, Algiers, Tunis, and Tripoli to send state-supported pirates to capture ships and hostages. The United States, then, offered easier targets than did England and France, because the United States had no navy. Attacks began, and "in 1785, Dey Muhammad of Algiers declared war on the United States and captured several American ships. The financially troubled Confederation Government of the United States was unable to raise a navy or the tribute that would protect U.S. ships. In

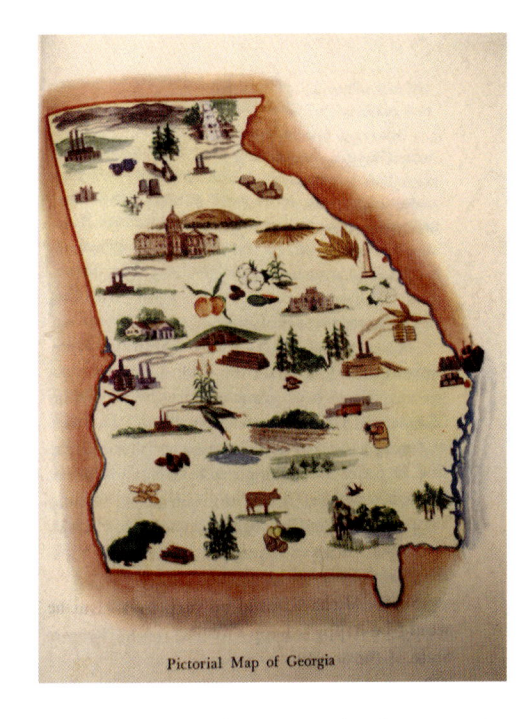

Pictorial Map of Georgia

contrast to the dispute with Algiers, U.S. negotiations with Morocco went well. Moroccan Sultan Sidi Muhammad had seized a U.S. merchant ship in 1784 after the United States had ignored diplomatic overtures. However, Muhammad ultimately followed a policy of peaceful trade, and the United States successfully concluded a treaty with Morocco in 1786. The adoption of the Constitution in 1789 gave the U.S. Government the power to levy taxes and to raise and maintain armed forces, powers that had been lacking under the Articles of Confederation. Once the Treaty of Ghent ended the war with England, President James Madison requested that Congress declare war on Algiers, with Congress authorizing the use of force on March 3, 1815. The U.S. Navy, greatly increased in size after the War of 1812, was able to send an entire squadron, led by Commodore Stephen Decatur, to the Mediterranean. Decatur quickly defeated two Algerian warships and captured hundreds of prisoners of war and

Above: Georgia often named counties for military heroes. Stephen Decatur (1779-1820) served in the American Revolution and the Barbary Wars. Georgia named Decatur County for him in 1823. This portrait of Decatur is attributed to artist Charles Bird King after Gilbert Stuart and hangs in the National Gallery of Art in Washington, DC.

was in a favorable position for negotiation. Dey Omar reluctantly accepted the treaty proposed by Decatur that called for an exchange of U.S. and Algerian prisoners, and an end to the practices of tribute and ransom. Having defeated the most powerful of the Barbary States, Decatur sailed to Tunis and Tripoli and obtained similar treaties. In Tripoli, Decatur also secured from Pasha Qaramanli the release of all European captives. The United States successfully defeated Qaramanli's forces with a combined naval and land assault by the United States Marine Corps." ("Barbary Wars, 1801-1805 and 1815-1816")

Incidentally, Decatur County and Decatur, Georgia are named for Commodore Stephen Decatur.

Even before the end of the American Revolution, George Washington and Thomas Jefferson saw the immediate need for a navy and looked, among other places, to the southeast coast of Georgia for raw materials to build it: "On Friday, October 13, 1775, meeting in Philadelphia, the Continental Congress voted to fit out two sailing vessels, armed with ten carriage guns, as well as swivel guns, and manned by crews of eighty, and to send them out on a cruise of three months to intercept transports carrying munitions and stores to the British army in America. This was the original legislation out of which the Continental Navy grew, and as such constitutes the birth certificate of the navy." ("The Birth of the Navy of the United States")

Then on March 27, 1794, Washington signed the *Act to Provide a Naval Armament* authorizing "the creation of six frigates to protect America from 'the depredations committed by the Algerine corsairs on the commerce of the United States.'" (Brooks)

Seeking to further unify the nation, Washington authorized raw materials from Maine, the Carolinas, and Georgia, and engaged shipyards in Philadelphia, Boston, New York, Gosport (now Norfolk), Fells Point (a suburb of Baltimore), and Portsmouth (New Hampshire). *The USS President, USS Constellation, USS Chesapeake, USS United States, USS Congress,* and *the USS Constitution* served during the Barbary Wars and the War of 1812. The *USS Constitution* still graces Boston Harbor. She defeated the British warships *HMS Guerriere, HMS Java, HMS*

Manufacturing Success in Georgia

Old Ironsides by Oliver Wendell Holmes, Sr.

Ay, tear her tattered ensign down!
Long has it waved on high,
Any many an eye has danced to see
That banner in the sky;
Beneath it rung the battle shout,
And burst the cannon's roar;
The meteor of the ocean air
Shall sweep the clouds no more!

Her deck, once red with heroes' blood
Where knelt the vanquished foe,
When winds were hurrying o're the flood
And waves were white below,
No more shall feel the victor's tread,
Or know the conquered knee;
The harpies of the shore shall pluck
The eagle of the sea!

Oh, better that her shattered hulk
Should sink beneath the wave;
Her thunders shook the mighty deep,
And there should be her grave;
Nail to the mast her holy flag,
Set every threadbare sail,
And give her to the god of storms,
The lightning and the gale!

Pictou, HMS Cyane, HMS Levant, and several merchant vessels.

In September 1830, Oliver Wendell Holmes, Sr. read a newspaper article stating that the *USS Constitution* was slated for destruction. In opposition, he wrote the poem "Old Ironsides", which was published in newspapers. The ship gained this nickname when cannonballs seemed to bounce off her hull without damaging it. The Constitution's hull, built from Georgia Live Oak, was strong wood, and had been cut with the grain, minimizing joints. Live Oak "timber has a density of 75 pounds per cubic foot, making it heavier than water, heavier than most other common timbers. The huge internal braces of the ship were cut in solid pieces from individual trees, as opposed to being compositely joined on site. The result was a hard body that appeared to deflect cannonballs like iron." (Brooks)

U.S. Timber Surveyor James Gould (1772 –1852) originally from Granville, Massachusetts, chose Live Oak limbs for the ship's construction on St. Simon's Island, Georgia. The center mast came from the Georgia property of Scotsman John Couper (1759 –1850). After surveying

CHAPTER 2

Right: The interior of Christ Church on St. Simons is built like the hull of a ship.

lumber to build the USS Constitution, Gould stayed on St. Simons and was contracted to build its first lighthouse in 1804. Couper's Cannon Point plantation became Cannon's Point Preserve, "a 600-acre tract of greenspace at the north end of St. Simons Island open for public exploration," when the final land purchase closed on September 28, 2012, and features "wild native species, beautiful mature maritime forest, and six miles of marsh-upland interface." ("Cannon's Point Preserve")

The *USS Constitution,* once scheduled for destruction and salvaging but saved by Oliver Wendell Holmes, Sr.'s poem *Old Ironsides,* still sits in Boston Harbor, while Gould's and Couper's remains lie in Christ Church Cemetery on St. Simon's Island. The current Christ Church building was constructed using timber money from the nineteenth century Dodge Family lumber mill operation on the island. Its interior is designed like the interior of a ship. The *USS Constitution* led the parade of tall ships in Boston Harbor on July 10, 1976, to celebrate The United States' Bicentennial.

DIVERSITY

Manufacturing in Georgia was also influenced by the people who made this part of the New World their home. Native Americans were here first. While questions remain about who discovered America, there is no doubt that the indigenous peoples were here before the European explorers many of us learned about in elementary school. Early twentieth-century performer Will Rogers commented about his experience in obtaining a passport. *The Dallas Morning News* quoted him in 1926 and then Rogers added the jest to his act. He said, "I never had my Americanism doubted before. My mother and my father both were part Cherokee Indian. Of course, my people didn't come over on the *Mayflower* but we were there to meet the folks when they landed." (*Quote Investigator*)

Manufacturing Success in Georgia

> **Now and Then:**
>
> With new mirgrations of people, per Georgia's land distribution lotteries, came new ways of accomplishing everyday tasks
>
> As time progressed, crafting became industry, and industry became manufacturing. Manufacturing adds value to raw materials by physically or chemically transforming them into new products. Cotton provides an example: a farmer plants and harvests cotton, a gin removes the seeds, a loom produces cloth. This becomes manufacturing when the production volume increases, and machinery is used to meet market demands. Modern manufacturing strives for safe working environments and control of environmental pollutants. In 2017, Richard Z. Lawrence wrote "Does Manufacturing Have the Largest Employment 'Multiplier' for the Domestic Economy?" for *Peterson Institute for International Economics.*
>
> In the article, he says that:
>
> - Each manufacturing job creates or supports three to four other jobs in the wider economy, which is five to seven indirect jobs, many of them in service industries, through the so-called "multiplier effect". That is, wages from manufacturing employees are re-spent in other parts of the economy: "Reports from the Manufacturing Institute indicate that each dollar's worth of manufactured goods creates another $1.34 of value elsewhere in the economy. This is the largest 'multiplier' of any sector. The impression sometimes given by such claims is that a dollar spent on manufacturing will 'create' more employment opportunities than a dollar spent on services." (Lawrence)
>
> - Technological advances in manufacturing machinery and equipment generate Productivity in workers, and spur economic growth by about three percent per year.
>
> - Trade with other countries centers on manufactured goods.
>
> - Service industries depend upon manufacturing. These include warehousing, logistics, distribution, transportation, retail, insurance, marketing, and financial institutions.
>
> - Industrial machinery generates national wealth which finances national defense. The United States, China, Japan, Great England, France, and Russia lead in manufacturing, therefore they wield power in global affairs.
>
> - A strong manufacturing culture strengthens the middle class of a society whose buying power fuels the national economy.

Each group of people impacted what Georgia would become in terms of crafting, industry, and manufacturing. Since archeological records indicate human habitation in what is now Georgia as early as 13,000 BC, Europeans first entered trading activities with the people they encountered, the great mound builders. These nations built earthen mounds on which to locate their temples and the homes of their leaders. To learn more about this history, visit *Etowah Mounds* State Historic Site near Cartersville, Ocmulgee *National Park and Preserve at Macon, and Kolomoki Mounds* State Park near *Blakely,* Georgia. Early European trading forts, called factories and built as early as the 1600s, dotted the landscape.

Although Christopher Columbus never made it to what we now call the United States, Giovanni Caboto, whose name was Anglicized to John Cabot, claimed Newfoundland and the continent for England in 1498. Lucas Vazquez de Ayllon, however, came to the South Carolina and Georgia coasts and established a colony in 1526. Most experts place the colony near today's Sapelo Island in McIntosh County, but South Carolina also claims it. Vazquez de Ayllon named his adventure San Miguel de Gualdape, but the ill-fated colony disintegrated soon after his death, only a few months after its establishment. Of the six hundred people who set out to colonize the American south, only one hundred fifty survived to return home.

The Spanish next sent Hernando de Soto through Georgia and other areas of the south in a 1539–1542 expedition. Just as Vazquez's death ended the early Spanish colony in Georgia, DeSoto's death ended this early exploration. Pedro Menendez de Aviles founded St. Augustine, Florida, in 1565. European contact with the indigenous peoples devastated their populations because the natives were not immune to common European ailments. By the time Oglethorpe arrived and ended Spanish inroads to Georgia in the 1700s, the mound builders were gone, and the natives had realigned themselves into the Muskogee and Cherokee tribes most Georgians recognize today. With Oglethorpe came settlers "from a vast array of regions around the Atlantic basin—including the British Isles, northern Europe, the Mediterranean, Africa, the Caribbean, and a host of American colonies. They arrived in very different social and economic circumstances, bringing preconceptions and cultural practices from their homelands. Each wave of immigrants changed the character of the colony—its size, composition, and economy—and brought new opportunities and new challenges to the people already there. Highland Scots settled a Celtic outpost at Darien on the southern frontier. Lutheran Salzburgers swiftly organized a productive and dutiful township at Ebenezer to the north. English folk, many of them Londoners, dominated Savannah and its surrounding villages, along with a large number of Rhineland Germans and a few Lowland Scots. In and around these regional settlements were smaller enclaves of immigrants, including Spanish-speaking Sephardic Jews, French-speaking Swiss, pious Moravians, Irish convicts, and a handful of Piedmont Italians and Russians." (Marsh)

By 1805, Georgia had set up a system of Land Lotteries to encourage settlement. The Lottery system (1805-1833) encouraged settlement, rewarded those who supported an independent and expanding United States, and brought people with various crafting and manufacturing skills here: "By 1820, civilians meeting certain qualifications, soldiers of Indian Wars, invalid or indigent veterans of the Revolutionary War and the War of 1812, widows of soldiers in those wars and orphans of soldiers in those wars were eligible to apply. By 1832, lands once occupied by Native Americans

Manufacturing Success in Georgia

Left: Western saddles similar to those produced by Bona Allen: many of Bona Allen's sales were used by mid-twentieth-century television cowboys.

forced out of Georgia on the infamous Trail of Tears were included. Thirty-one of Georgia's 159 counties granted lands in the lotteries: Appling, Baldwin, Bartow, Carroll, Cherokee, Cobb, Coweta, Dooly, Early, Fayette, Floyd, Forsyth, Gilmer, Gwinnett, Habersham, Hall, Henry, Houston, Irwin, Lee, Lumpkin, Monroe, Murray, Muscogee, Paulding, Rabun, Troup, Union, Walton, Wayne, and Wilkinson. One famous Revolutionary War hero who received Georgia lands in partial payment for his services was Major General *Nathanael Greene* (1742 – 19 June 1786)." (Woods)

Interesting fact, General Greene's widow, Catherine, introduced the ideas to Eli Whitney, which prompted him to invent the cotton gin (more details in Chapter 3).

THE BONA ALLEN COMPANY

Bona Allen's story shows that manufacturing begins with crafting. Founded in 1873 by Bonaparte Allen, Sr. and headquartered in Buford, Bona Allen made saddles, handbags, cowboy boots, and shoes. The tannery prepared materials for Spaulding baseballs and baseball mitts. The Great Depression, World War I, and World War II helped Bona Allen, because more people used horses and mules when gasoline was in short supply, increasing the need for saddle production. The United States also contracted the company to produce and repair military footwear. In the 1920s and 1930s, Bona Allen manufactured over three thousand pairs of shoes daily. In the 1940s, the

Right: The illustration shows a Bona Allen advertisement for shoes. It is preserved and on display at the Museum of Buford.

company produced four thousand shoes a day. During World War II, the company repaired or refurbished approximately six thousand pairs of military shoes per day under the guidance of the U.S. Army Quartermaster Corps. *Vintage Gun Leather* website posted that "Modern machinery was evident throughout the tannery division, but a great deal of hand labor was still necessary for converting tough, stiff, hair-covered cowhides into smooth, flexible sheets of leather. In the harness factory, a designation carried over from the heyday of the horse and buggy, the majority of the plant was devoted to manufacturing riding equipment. Here, highly skilled craftsmen and women painstakingly cut, stitched, and hand-tooled the high-quality Bona Allen leather especially made to withstand rugged use. Saddles, bridles, halters, harnesses, stirrups, and a dozen or more different kinds of riding accessories were cut and assembled in this section."

Another phenomenon that pushed Bona Allen to success was the American Western television shows of the 1950s. Favorite series included *The Lone Ranger, The Rifleman, Bonanza, Daniel Boone, Branded, The Guns of Will Sonnett, Gunsmoke, The Wild Wild West, The Big Valley, Cheyenne, The Cisco Kid, Laredo, The Life and Legend of Wyatt Earp, Rawhide, The Virginian, Wagon Train,* and *The Roy Rogers Show*. Stephen Kiss, Sr. of the New York Public Library writes that "Before television, the nation saw Westerns at movie theaters and listened to them over the radio. When Westerns started appearing on TV, viewers avidly waited for their favorites. In any one week, Westerns often received the highest viewer ratings. Viewers were able to escape their humdrum lives to watch their favorite heroes overcome all adversaries. It was good vs. bad, hero vs. villain, in the old nineteenth-century West. But it was much more than that. Early TV Western series helped define America as a

Manufacturing Success in Georgia

nation. Westerns sought to teach the good values of honesty and integrity, of hard work, of racial tolerance, determination to succeed, and of justice for all. They were, in a sense, modern morality plays where heroes, strong, reliable, clear-headed, and decent, fought their adversaries in the name of justice. At the show's end, moral lessons had been taught and learned."

Because viewers loved Westerns, actors needed saddles and saddlebags. Bona Allen made custom saddles for Western actors, singers, and showmen Roy Rogers, William F. "Buffalo Bill" Cody, Gene Autry, Kenny Rogers, Lash LaRue, Gabby Hayes, and the cast of the popular television show *Bonanza* starring *Georgia-born* Pernell Roberts as Adam Cartwright.

Saddle expert Victor Allen left the famous King Ranch in Texas to lead the saddle division of Bona Allen during this time, when actors frequently brought their horses to Buford for a custom fit. These hand-crafted works of art led the way for Bona Allen to mass-produce products to be sold at Sears. A monument depicting Roy Rogers, his stallion Trigger, and Bona Allen saddle maker Jack Johnson now stands in downtown Buford. In 1968, Tandy Corporation bought Bona Allen. It operated until 1981, when investors moved into the technology market and fire razed part of the property. In 2005, Buford had the main tannery building placed on the National Register of Historic Places. When another fire occurred in 2015,

Now and Then:

Georgia's public schools used this 1956 *Our Georgia* text by Louise Maynard and Ruth Wynn Aultman in fourth grade throughout the 1960s. Elizabeth Rice illustrated the Georgia map that thousands of students remember. It shows manufacturing and industry sites in what was then called "The Empire State". Manufacturing moves crafting to mechanized production and high yields.

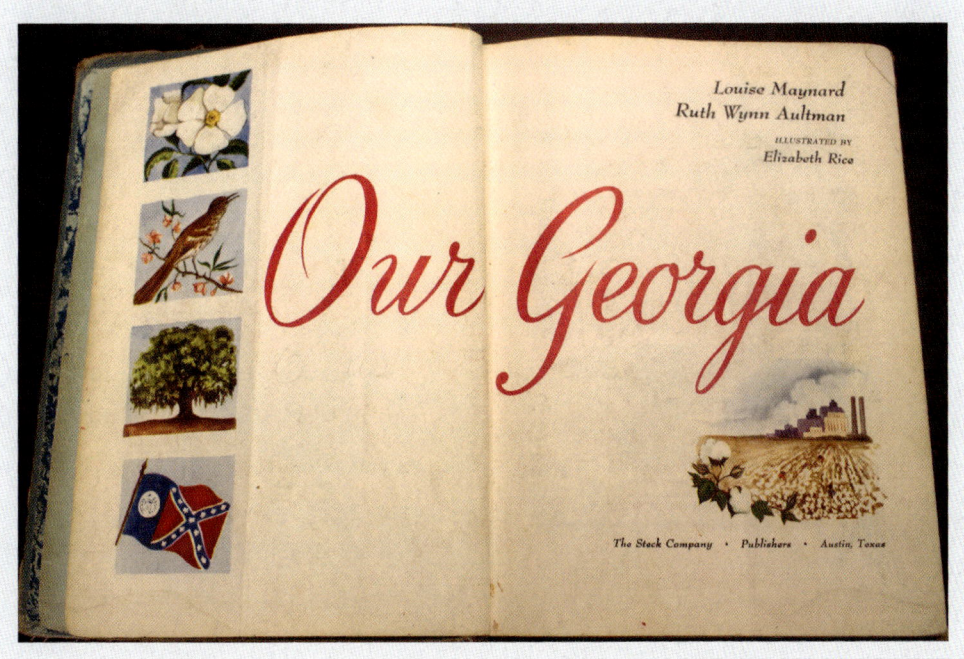

Now and Then (continued):

Today's Georgia looks a little different. The Georgia Manufacturing Industry Database (MNI) and Georgia Manufacturer's Register provides these statistics for 2020-2021.

Largest Georgia Manufacturers by Employees:

Gulfstream Aerospace Corp. (Savannah) - *10,000*

Lockheed Martin Aeronautics Co. (Marietta) - *6,200*

Coca-Cola Co., The (Atlanta) - *5,000*

Mohawk Industries, Inc., Aladdin Div. (Dalton) - *3,255*

Georgia-Pacific, LLC (Atlanta) - *3,200*

Leading Georgia Industries by Employment:

15% Food and kindred products

10% Transportation equipment

9% Industrial machinery and equipment

9% Textile mill products

7% Rubber and miscellaneous plastic products

Georgia Counties with the Most Manufacturing Jobs:

Fulton - *105,726*

Gwinnett - *44,841*

Cobb - *33,469*

Whitfield - *23,321*

Chatham - *20,901*

Georgia Cities with the Most Manufacturing Jobs:

Atlanta - *70,029*

Dalton - *23,119*

Alpharetta - *22,664*

Savannah - *18,706*

Norcross - *15,703*

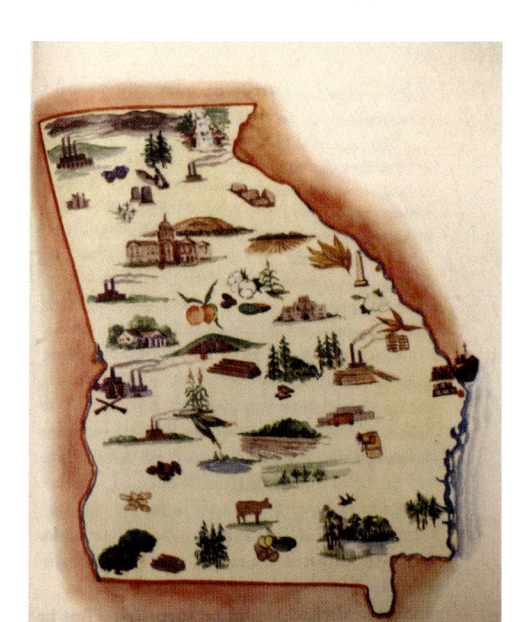

Pictorial Map of Georgia

firefighters contained the blaze but allowed the structure to burn itself to the ground.

Bona Allen's legacy of leather works and shoemaking also made Buford the natural place for follow-on manufacturing, Bradshaw writes for *Patch*, a local breaking news site. She says, "Just before the 1920s, the Bona Allen tannery, which had long been providing material for horse collars, saddles, and other products, found a new outlet for its scrap leather – shoes. A separate factory for shoe production was built in 1919, increasing both employment for the town, and profit for the Allens. During the 1920s and '30s, the Bona Allen Shoe Factory produced over 3,000 pairs of shoes daily, which were sold and shipped all over the country. Although

Manufacturing Success in Georgia

the factory produced some military and everyday footwear, it also branched out and made men's dress shoes. The factory prospered for two decades, including the depression years. In 1940 the *Blue Book of the Leather and Shoe Industry* reported that Bona Allen Shoes had a Capital and Surplus of $2,000,000, a daily output of 4,000 shoes, and even had a branch office in New York City. Shoes included men's, women's, and youth's medium welts, and nailed shoes; misses welts; also children's and infant's stitchdowns. Trademark shoes included the 'Bona Allen Shoe,' 'The Victor Five,' and the 'Bobby Burns.'" (Bradshaw)

OKABASHI

By 1984, Buford had a new shoe company following in Bona Allen's footsteps: Okabashi. "Over 99% of American-worn footwear is made abroad. We are proud to be in the 1% that chose to stay and thrive in the USA. With over 35 million pairs of shoes sold, Okabashi's flip flops and sandals focus on foot health and wellness with comfort as the key to a healthy and active lifestyle. We design shoes that promote foot health and comfort with active arch support, massage beads, and a two-year guarantee. The company operates in a 100,000-square-foot facility and partners with local vendors where possible. Okabashi has donated over 100,000 pairs of shoes for disaster relief, veterans, and more." (*Okabashi*)

On April 4, 2020, Kiersten Willis wrote in the *Atlanta Journal-Constitution* that, "In an effort to support health care workers on the front line of the coronavirus pandemic, Georgia-based Okabashi Brands has launched a new campaign. The Comfort for Frontline Heroes campaign will donate shoes to the medical professionals working amid the outbreak."

Right: Eli Whitney's Cotton Gin (Library of Congress)

CHAPTER 3

COTTON IS KING

Textile Manufacturing, The Cotton Gin, and The Battlefield: Jefferson Mills, Lummus, Tift Mills and the Young Children, Standard Textile, Bibb Manufacturing, Jarrell Plantation and Griswoldville

COTTON AND THE COTTON GIN

Cotton grew well in Georgia, but transitioning Upland, or short fiber cotton, to cloth was a labor-intensive process. The introduction of Sea Island Cotton, which had a longer, silkier fiber, made textile production much more profitable. The invention of the cotton gin and the legalization of slave labor changed cotton production dramatically. At its foundation, Georgia grew rice and indigo, harvested timber, and collected Naval Stores. Hard manual labor, without the benefit of mechanization, was the rule. The importation of African slaves was banned until 1751. Woods writes that "The entire American cotton crop in the 1780s grew on less than two hundred acres, virtually all of them located in the Sea Islands of South Carolina and Georgia. Spinning a pound of cotton thread by hand, thanks to its natural twist, took far longer than spinning wool, linen, or even silk, between twelve and fourteen man-days in all. Only five hundred thousand pounds of cotton was spun into thread – all by hand – in 1765."

As Georgia, the last of the original thirteen colonies, moved from the control of a Board of Trustees to direct rule by the king, legalized and wide-spread slavery gained ground. Only wealthy landowners could choose to purchase slaves. The average farmer grew only enough cotton to support his family, and possibly worked for a wealthy landowner. Thus, the plantation culture grew. In 1790, the cultivation of Sea Island Cotton began in South Carolina and Georgia. Then in 1793, Eli Whitney invented the cotton gin. Shortly thereafter, "Cotton was King." Around 1800, "sixteen million pounds of cotton were spun, by machine, and the price of cotton cloth had dropped. A field hand could pick about fifty pounds of cotton in a day, enough eventually to yield about four pounds of cotton 'lint' ready for spinning. But removing the seeds from that much cotton took a single worker fully twenty-five days." (Woods). Whitney's hand-cranked cotton gin removed the seeds from fifty pounds of cotton per day, and horse-powered or machine-driven gins worked even faster.

Another factor in the invention of the cotton gin was the direct result of new settlers coming to Georgia through a land lottery system. Lands previously owned by Native Americans and acquired by

Above: Three stages of cotton in the field: the blossom, the bulb, and the boll.

CHAPTER 3

21

Above: A modern cotton picker replaces three workers, and the older rectangular bales which weighed about 500 pounds. The new cotton picker rolls the cotton into 4,200-pound bundles that go to the gin. Other farmers pack their cotton into modules that weigh approximately 14,000 pounds.

treaty or government regulation were divided and offered, in many cases, to veterans of the Revolutionary War and the War of 1812: One famous Revolutionary War hero who received Georgia lands in partial payment for his services was Major General Nathanael Greene (1742 – 1786). It was on his Mulberry Grove plantation near Savannah that Eli Whitney invented the cotton gin in 1793. Oral history about the invention says that General Greene's widow, Catherine Littlefield Greene Miller (1755 – 1814), and Eli Whitney shared a casual conversation about a hairbrush which inspired the idea to brush or comb the seeds from cotton.

The cotton ginning process involved combs and brushes that pulled seeds from cotton bolls. The ginned cotton was shipped to factories for the production of clothing, medical supplies, carpet, and other applications. Woods wrote for *Mechanical Engineering* that even the seeds find their way to market as "cottonseed oil, which is used in cooking and candy making. Seeds are used in such widely assorted applications as cattle feed, paper, and as a source of cellulose for making nitrocellulose."

Ginned cotton is pressed into bales and sealed in plastic, then loaded onto trucks for transport. Photographs were taken in January 2020. Older equipment, from Pitts Gin, was sold to an expanding cotton industry in South America.

Whitney's gin was simple, and copied by other inventors. He prospered with further inventions, and is often credited with developments leading to mass production: "In Whitney's gin a roller studded with nails stripped the lint from the seeds by pulling it through a grid too narrow to let the seeds pass. The seeds fell into one compartment, and a brush swept the lint off the nails and into another compartment. Whitney's machine could be built in an hour or so by any competent carpenter, and worked by a single laborer, increasing his productivity

Manufacturing Success in Georgia

Trucks take the cotton to gins. Machinery moves the cotton from bales and the gin removes the first seeds.

fully fifty times. In a stroke, Whitney had reduced the labor cost of ginning from the dominant component in the cost of cotton cloth to a near triviality. The South, able to grow cotton very profitably at a much lower price than ever before (or anywhere else), became the natural empire of 'King Cotton' as the demand of the British and New England mills became insatiable." (Gordon)

Quickly, gins and textile mills became leading industries, first in the northeast, and then in the southeast: "A major force in cotton economy, textile mills grew throughout the United States from around 1860 to 1900. This happened in part due to the Industrial Revolution, and in the south, in response to losing vast tracts of cotton farms and the labor which made growing cotton profitable.

In short, farmers became factory workers. Mill villages sprang up. In Georgia, these included Lamar County's Aldora, Bibb County's Payne City, and Colquitt County's Riverside. These communities maintained a separate government than their surrounding cities, provided special activities and educational opportunities for mill workers' children, and developed unique cultures with tight-knit families. Some researchers even describe the mills as paternalistic." (Wickersham and Yehl)

Payne City maintained elements of its self-government from 1899, until it was dissolved by an act of the Georgia Legislature in 2015, long after mill closure.

JEFFERSON MILLS

Jefferson Mills, located in Jefferson City, Georgia, was one of the first textile mills challenged by the U.S. Government for their claim of parental expenditures on their tax return. In the Jefferson Mills, Inc. v. United States case (1965), the mill claimed "ordinary and necessary business expenses" but the government

CHAPTER 3

determined that the expenditures were charitable donations and allowed only a percentage to count as deductions. Upon the depositions of W. L. Colombo, Joseph H. Porter, Thomas M. Bryan, II, and Morris Marion Bryan, Jr., Jefferson Mills explained that their employees needed a higher level of education. They could move the company, build and maintain their school, or supplement the local public-school system. They chose to supplement the local schools as a cost-efficient way to keep the community and mill employees in a unified community, and eventually hired about fifty percent of new workers from the public schools.

The case came to trial in United States District Court N. D. Georgia, Gainesville Division when "Jefferson Mills was the largest employer in the City of Jefferson, Georgia, ... a city with a population of approximately 1750 persons" (The JEFFERSON MILLS, INC. v. UNITED STATES of America [1965]).

The final decision favored the mills:

Here the taxpayer, because of the inferior local school, decided that it was confronted with three choices, one of which it must accept. (1) Plaintiff could move its plant to someplace with better educational facilities, or (2) it could put in a school of its own, or (3) it could contract with the Board for the upgrading of the Jefferson City School.

The taxpayer's officers decided that the last alternative was most desirable, and approved the offered contract. This was a valid decision, and the payments made under such a contract were properly treated as ordinary and necessary business expenses as that term is used in § 162(a) of the Internal Revenue Code of 1954.

There being no genuine dispute as to any material fact, the plaintiff's motion for summary judgment is granted, and the defendant's motion for summary judgment is denied.

The defendant is directed to have the amount of refund due to the plaintiff hereunder properly computed by the Internal Revenue Service so that it may be made a part of the judgment in which the Court hereby directs be prepared and presented. (The JEFFERSON MILLS, INC. v. UNITED STATES of America [1965])

LUMMUS

Franklin Hadley Lummus established the New York Cotton Gin Company in 1863. A series of partnerships and company purchases made the company what it is today. Lummus' sons, E. Frank and Louis E. moved the company to Juniper, Georgia, and later to Columbus, Georgia: "By 1910, they bought Air Blast Gin Company and expanded to form Lummus Cotton Gin Company. Their innovations led the industry. Lummus was an early leader in developing machinery for man-made fiber, too. The company quickly realized that traditional machinery would not work for synthetics and developed processing that would. Their methods became industry standards. Growth continued and the company became Lummus Industries, Inc. in 1969 and then Lummus Corporation in 1993. In 1999, the company moved to

Above: Franklin Hadley Lummus from New Georgia Encyclopedia

Savannah for expansion and to be closer to the ships that would take their products around the world." (Lummus: History)

Today, Lummus supplies machinery and replacement parts for cotton ginning worldwide, using brand names Lummus Consolidated and Beltwide. They also provide aftermarket parts for oilseed, and food processing and machinery for synthetic fiber production, named Carver and Gump. Lummus Australia Pty., Ltd in Moree, New South Wales and Lummus Do Brasil, Ltda. in Cioba, Mato Grosso serve as subsidiary companies. Parts production, sales centers, and warehouses that serve the United States are located in Lake Village, Arkansas; Memphis, Tennessee; Casa Grande, Arizona; Harlingen, Texas; and Fresno, California. The corporate headquarters and primary manufacturing operations are in Savannah, Georgia.

Above: Lummus 4/170-Saw Imperial™ III Gin Plant

Left: Lummus Cotton Gins: (Georgia State Historic Markers)

LUMMUS COTTON GINS

On this site in 1847 stood the E. T. Taylor Cotton Gin Manufacturing Company. In 1854 it became the W. G. Clemons, Brown & Company and operated as such until the Civil War. In 1867 Franklin H. Lummus controlled the company and the name "Lummus" became synonymous with the manufacture of cotton gins. The company moved to Juniper, Georgia but returned to Columbus in 1899. Lummus Cotton Gin Company became the world's largest independent gin manufacturer. Diversification into textile machinery and man-made fiber equipment was reflected in a name change to Lummus Industries, Incorporated in 1970.

In 1993, a new company, Lummus Corporation, was formed to purchase certain assets from the bankrupt Lummus Industries. Today, Lummus Corporation is the premiere manufacturer of cotton ginning equipment.

CHAPTER 3

Above: Two of the "helpers" in the Tifton Cotton Mill, Tifton, Ga. They work regularly, 1909. Eddie Lou Young at right, 8 years old. Tifton, Georgia, January 22, 1909.

Above: A family working the the Tifton (Ga.) Cotton Mill. Mrs. A.J. Young works in mill and at home. Nell (oldest girl) alternates in mill with mother. Manny (next girl) runs 2 sides. Mary (next) runs 1 1/2 sides. Elic (oldest boy) works regularly. Eddit (next girl) helps in mill, sticks on bobbins. Four smallest children not working yet. The mother said she earns $4.50 a week and all the children earn $4.50 a week. Husband died and left her 11 children. 2 of them went off and got married. The family left the farm 2 years ago to work in the mill. January 22, 1909. Location: Tifton, Georgia.

TIFTON COTTON MILL AND THE YOUNG CHILDREN

Human interest is another side of the mill and gin story. What started as an exhibit of five photos taken by Lewis Hine in 1905 led to a reunion of "over 100 relatives (descendants of the cotton mill children in the five original photos) who had never met before and didn't even realize they were related until 2011." (Press Release on Tift Cotton Mill Discovery: Georgia The Georgia Museum of Agriculture & Historic Village, 2011)

Massachusetts researcher Joe Manning found the first photo, and later matched the brunette child to the second Hines photo labeled "Mrs. A.J. Young Family". It shows nine of her eleven children. He followed the story of Eddie Lou Young, aged eight at the time of the photo, and her brothers and sisters, as they moved off the farm after the death of their father, and worked in the Tifton Cotton Mill to help their mother support the family. Before long, the family could not support themselves and several of the children went to orphanages. Manning traced descendants, and in 2011, over 100 of them met at The Georgia Museum of Agriculture & Historic Village exhibit to talk about their family history. A workshop after the opening session taught participants how to gather and display their family histories. Abraham Baldwin Agricultural College partners with the museum for such events.

STANDARD TEXTILE

Another human interest story is that of Charles Heimen, who escaped from Dachau, the first Nazi concentration camp, opened in 1933, shortly after Adolf Hitler (1889-1945) became chancellor of Germany. Heimen immigrated to the United States and founded Standard Textiles with his family. The German immigrants established the company from a third-floor apartment on July 1, 1940, in Cincinnati: "All of the companies' original employees were also refugees." (Standard Textile)

By 1945, they moved the operation to a former shoe factory in the industrial district. By 1963, Standard Textile needed a world headquarters, and to choose a larger site in Cinncinati. Soon, Standard expanded to Thomaston, Georgia. They became international manufacturers with the establishment of a mill in Arad, Israel in the 1970s. Their greatest contributions are in healthcare fabrics such as ComPel fabric, which became the industry standard. Currently, Standard Textile produces healthcare fabrics for "the United States and 32 other countries around the globe." (Standard Textile).

The family legacy continues. When Charles retired, his son Paul took the reins leading "4,000 committed associates at 24 manufacturing, distribution, and sales facilities ... to serve customers in more than 90 international markets." (Standard Textile)

The company produces fabric for "healthcare, hospitality, interiors, and workwear," (Standard Textile) and today, holds over eighty patents, and employs thousands of workers.

BIBB MANUFACTURING

Bibb Manufacturing Company began in 1876 in Macon, Georgia. It became one of Georgia's largest mid-twentieth century employers, but declined by the 1990s.

Left: Working in a Cotton Mill (Library of Congress)

Cotton merchant Hugh Moss Comer, Major John F. Hanson, and I. Newton Hanson started the company. Arden Williams wrote about Bibb Manufacturing for the *New Georgia Encyclopedia*: "By 1895 the Bibb Manufacturing Company employed 700 workers and consumed 20,000 bales of cotton annually." The company expanded quickly. Williams writes that Bibb City in Columbus developed around 1900 "after Bibb Mills purchased land on the Chattahoochee

Left: Bibb Mill Workers (Library of Congress)

CHAPTER 3

27

Above: Payne City Textile Workers (Library of Congress)

River and built Columbus Mill, which "would become the largest cotton mill in the country. "By 1911 Bibb Manufacturing advertised itself as 'one of the largest and most important enterprises in the South.'" (Williams) The mill offered services for their workers to include free kindergarten and swimming pools: "Then in 1956 Robert Train, grandson of Hugh Comer, was appointed president. By this time textile mills all over the South were faltering. Bibb had acquired factories in other states but began to sell its company housing in the 1960s. By 1970, when William S. Manning became president, some of the factories were put up for sale. The succeeding decades saw more closures for Bibb. In 1996, under CEO Michael Fulbright, the Bibb Companies went through bankruptcy reorganization. Unable to recover economically, the company was sold in 1998 to the Dan River Corporation of Virginia. The mill communities, especially Bibb City, were affected by the closures. In 2000 Bibb City ceased to be an independent community, merging with the city of Columbus. Through its many products, employees, and mill communities, Bibb, known as 'the first name in textiles,' helped to shape Georgia during its many years of operation in the state." (Williams)

Paternalistic practices of mills for their employees provided schools, housing, commissaries (also called company stores where employees could purchase or charge to their accounts for anything from food to tools), churches, medical care; and in some cases, swimming pools, auditoriums, gymnasiums, athletic programs, extracurricular education programs for children while their parents worked, and youth clubs with company-paid social workers. One lady who grew up in Payne City, a mill village then surrounded by the City of Macon, reported fond memories of annual overnight field trips for teenagers, segregated by gender, of course.

JARRELL PLANTATION AND GRISWOLDVILLE

Georgia Historic Sites provides a timeline of moving raw materials from the farm to the factory at Jarrell Plantation near Juliette in Jones County. *"Dating back to*

Manufacturing Success in Georgia

Left: The Cotton and Lumber Mill at Jarrell Plantation

1847, through generations of family members, Jarrell Plantation Historic Site is one of the last remaining examples of a vanishing culture with its authentic nineteenth and early twentieth-century plantation buildings typical to Middle Georgia representing the change from an agricultural to an industrial-based economy." (Jarrell Plantation). The site was owned by one family for almost one hundred fifty years, and "survived General Sherman's 'March to the Sea,' typhoid fever, the cotton boll weevil, the advent of steam power, and a transition from farming to forestry."

John Fitz Jarrell began with a small farm that grew to nearly 1,000 acres. Then, "after John's death, his son, Dick Jarrell, gave up teaching to return to the farm, and in 1895, he built a small house for his family that grew to 12 children. Dick diversified the farm, adding a sawmill, cotton gin, gristmill, shingle mill, planer, a sugar cane press, syrup evaporator, workshop, barn, and outbuildings. In 1974, his descendants donated these buildings to establish Jarrell Plantation State Historic Site." *(Jarrell Plantation).*

Left: This Georgia made Griswold and Gunnison 1851 Navy Revolver is in the National Rifle Association (NRA) Museum, Fairfax, Virginia.

The reason General Sherman's men were in Mr. Jarrell's neighborhood was guns. Samuel Griswold (1790-1867), originally from Connecticut, came to Georgia and started a cotton gin, soap, and tallow factory, candle factory, sawmill, grist mill, post office and church along the railroad tracks near Clinton. In 1862, Griswold converted his factories to produce pikes and pistols. Fashioned after the Colt Navy 1851 revolver, the Griswold and Greer or Griswold Gunnison's revolvers are prized possessions of collectors today. Today, "Jarrell Plantation also maintains Griswoldville Battlefield, an unmanned seventeen-acre site where the Battle of Griswoldville happened on November 22, 1864." (Jarrell Plantation)

CHAPTER 3

Right: Catherine Evans Whitener - Courtesy of the Brandy Heritage Center of Northwest Georgia"

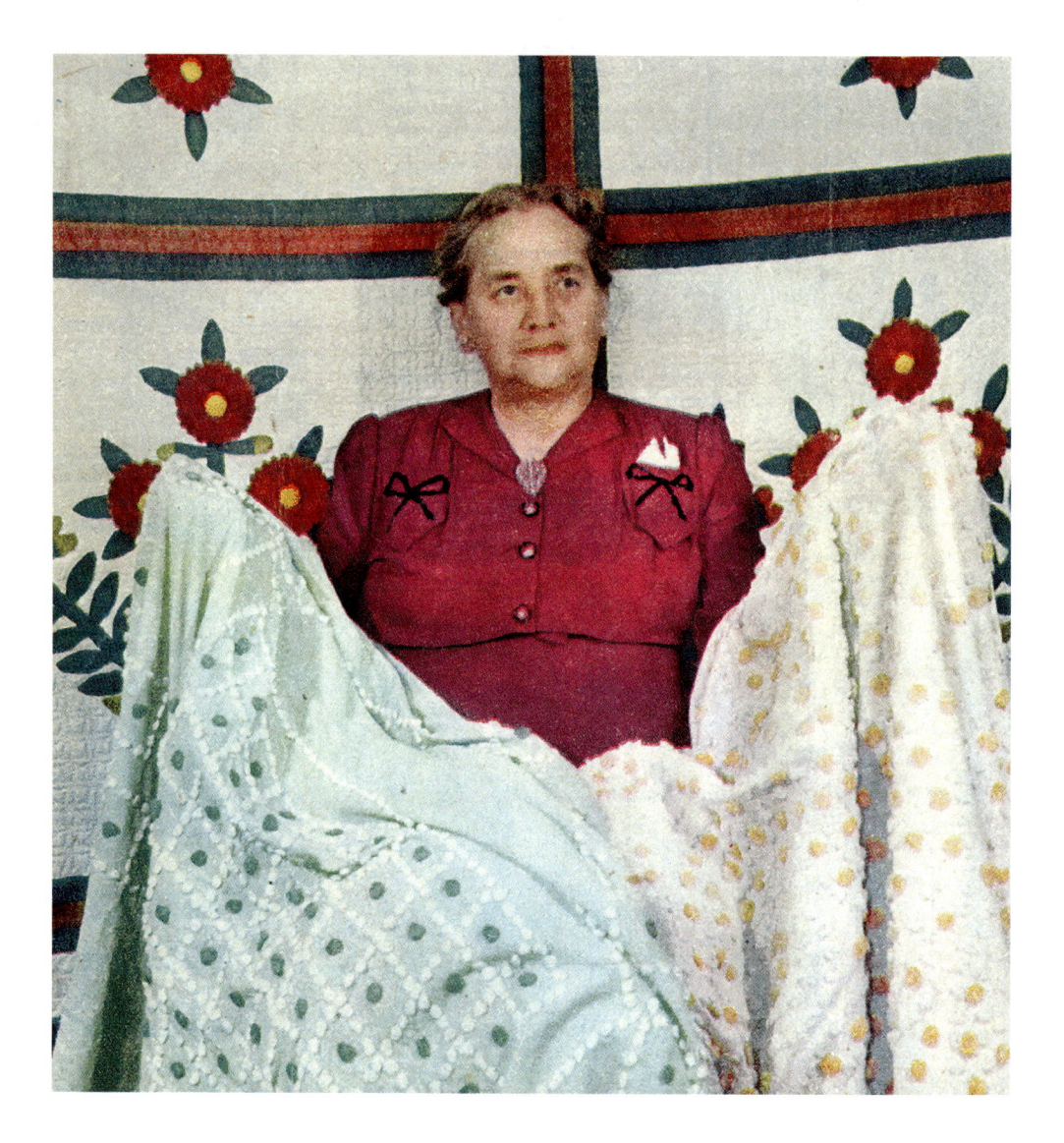

CHAPTER 4

TEXTILES, CARPET, AND FLOORING:

Shaw Industries, World Carpets, Beaulieu of America, Interface, Inc., J & J Industries, and Carpet Capital of the World

SHAW

Shaw Industries, a subsidiary of Berkshire Hathaway, is the world's largest carpet manufacturer. Located in Dalton, it also markets hardwood, vinyl, resilient flooring, laminate, tile, and stone. It helps retain Dalton's title of "Carpet Capital of the World". Randall L. Patton wrote for the *New Georgia Encyclopedia* that "Shaw Industries can trace its roots back to the old tufted, or chenille, bedspread industry that thrived in the Dalton area in the 1930s and 1940s."

Manufacturing Success in Georgia

Catherine Evans Whitener made chenille work popular in Dalton in the 1890s, by reviving an older tradition. This is another example in which crafting led to manufacturing. Cotton sheeting was tufted with thicker cotton yarn to form raised designs on bedspreads. The finished product is called chenille.

As the practice grew, people who produced these bedspreads hung them on clotheslines along Highway 41 to market to people traveling from the northeast coast to Florida: "The handcraft of tufting played an important role in the economic development of northwest Georgia. Evans and others who learned the technique stamped familiar patterns onto blank sheets, then filled the patterns with yarn. As the products grew in popularity, merchants in the Dalton region took an interest in marketing the spreads. By the 1920s chenille bedspreads appeared on the shelves of department stores in Atlanta, New York, Philadelphia, and other major cities." (Patton).

Left: Most chenille bedspreads used a white on white design. Manufacturing Success in Georgia shows dyed bedspreads here to highlight the detailed work in them.

Because the peacock pattern was so popular, travelers deemed the northwest Georgia section of Highway 41 "Peacock Alley".

When demand for chenille grew, merchants, such as Dalton's B. J. Bandy and Dicksie Bradley Bandy, printed designs on cotton sheeting and sent them to area farms for women to tuft. Finished crafts

CHAPTER 4

Right: The Putnam Family Chenille Shop on Peacock Alley

were then returned to factories for dyeing and finishing. Patton writes, "In the mid-1940s Clarence Shaw, a Georgia Institute of Technology graduate, started a firm to dye and finish small tufted products like bedspreads, robes, and small rugs. Shaw's Star Dye Company established a solid reputation and a stable clientele among makers of such products in the Dalton area." ("Shaw Industries")

Subsequent factory owners adapted sewing machines to tuft the fabric into chenille bedspreads, so what was once a cottage industry moved to manufacturing. Patton writes in "Carpet Industries" that, "In the 1930s and 1940s companies that had concentrated on manufacturing bedspreads introduced new products, including tufted robes, toilet seat and tank covers, and most importantly, small throw rugs (generally called scatter rugs in the trade)." The Dalton textile mills soon learned to adapt machines for heavier product, and the carpet industry was

Right: The Beckler Family Chenille Shop on Peacock Alley

Manufacturing Success in Georgia

born: "By the end of the 1950s, sales of bedspreads and other small tufted goods stagnated and began to decline, while the market for tufted carpets expanded by leaps and bounds." (Patton)

Dalton's history center, Crown Gardens and Archives, displays bedspreads from the period.

Clarence Shaw died in 1958, leaving the management of the family business to his sons, Robert E. and J. C. Shaw, who founded Star Finishing, and it "rose quickly and became the top commission finisher in the carpet industry by 1967." (Patton, "Shaw Industries")

The Shaw Industries website says, "Shaw got its start in 1946 as Star Dye Company, a small business that dyed tufted scatter rugs. The events that transformed the company into the world's largest carpet manufacturer are too numerous to write or even fully know." The company transformed its products through invention and machinery, and its business through consolidation.

Robert E. and J. C. Shaw acquired Philadelphia Carpet Company and established the Philadelphia Holding Company, which they renamed Shaw Industries in 1971. In the 1980s, "Shaw made a series of strategic moves that catapulted the firm to the top spot among carpet makers by a wide margin. Shaw opted in the early 1980s to compete with its largest customers—wholesale distributors. Distributors sold most of the carpet in the United States in 1980, and they extracted a sizable profit margin. Shaw boldly expanded its retail sales force, invested heavily in training, and went direct to small retailers. Shaw also integrated vertically in the 1980s, acquiring several yarn mills to reduce raw materials costs. With these and other calculated risks, Shaw rose to the top of the industry by 1986.

Later, the company acquired Cabin Crafts, a division of West Point Pepperell, and then several other competitors. They ventured into retail sales but "returned to its avowed core competencies—efficient manufacturing and effective service to retailers...Legendary investor Warren Buffett purchased a controlling interest in Shaw Industries in early 2001." (Patton, "Shaw Industry")

In 2020, with the leadership of CEO Vance Bell, Shaw is a full-service flooring company with nearly $6 billion in annual sales and approximately 22,000 employees.

WORLD CARPETS

In 1998, World Carpets merged with Mohawk Industries to create another of the nation's largest manufacturers of tufted carpets. The son of Palestinian immigrants, Shaheen Azeez Shaheen was a 1949 graduate of the Illinois Institute of Technology, who took a summer job in a rug mill at Dalton, Georgia. After graduation, he worked as a salesman for the same rug company in the Midwest and married "Piera Barbaglia, who was born in Mystic, Iowa, and raised in northern Italy. During World War II, Barbaglia, armed with a business degree, had managed the finances for the local underground movement against the Italian Fascists and German Nazis." (Deaton)

The New Georgia Encyclopedia article "World Carpets", by researcher Thomas M. Deaton, says that, "Barbaglia's expertise with finance and office management matched Shaheen's manufacturing experience and innovative marketing and labor skills." World Carpets spins and delivers finished products, and was one of the first companies in the industry to do so. They also raised manufacturing standards by meeting with Washington, D.C. officials to establish more stringent standards for Federal Housing Administration carpet contracts. The company offers "a profit-sharing program for all employees, bi-annual cash bonuses, educational scholarships for all employees' children, in-plant General Equivalency Diploma programs, and college tuition grants to employees." (Deaton)

The company also works to promote their community: they "have been active in the Stay in School program, the homeless rehabilitation program of Harvest Outreach, and worldwide evangelical missionary work." (Deaton).

BEAULIEU OF AMERICA

Beaulieu of America is an extension of a Belgium carpet company and is "the third-largest tufted carpet company in America," according to Deaton. Carl Bouckaert, the son-in-law of Roger De Clerck who owned Beaulieu Belgium, came to Georgia to visit "a company concentrating on the woven polypropylene Oriental rug market," with which De Clerck wished to expand their market. They first opened in Dalton, and later added a plant in Chatsworth.

In 1982, Bouckaert added polypropylene rug yarns to Beaulieu's offerings. The company acquired Barwick Carpets and established a partnership with D & W Carpets in Eton for outside yarns. Expansion continued with further acquisitions and expansions into Canada. Engineered Floors, owned by Robert E. Shaw, bought Beaulieu of America in 2017.

INTERFACE, INC.

Interface, Inc. of LaGrange specializes in commercial carpeting and is one of the world's largest manufacturers. Its annual revenues exceed $1 billion, and the company now has manufacturing facilities in the United States, the United Kingdom, and Australia. Interface has "become a leader in the movement for sustainable development, instituting pioneering environmental policies." (Patton, "Interface, Inc.")

Founded by Ray Anderson who holds a degree in industrial engineering from the

Manufacturing Success in Georgia

Georgia Institute of Technology, Interface is an example of long-term success.

Anderson "spent fourteen years, from the late 1950s through the early 1970s, working for Troup County's Callaway Mills and the firm that eventually bought Callaway, Deering-Milliken. While at Deering-Milliken, Anderson worked on a joint venture with Carpets International, a British firm." (Patton)

The firm developed carpet tiles that could be laid in patterns, and that did not use adhesive. This moved commercial carpet forward. It also helped carpets last longer, because now squares could be replaced, rather than an entire area of carpet.

Anderson began his new company by focusing on the technical process for making carpet tiles, called fusion bonding. The process implanted yarn directly into a piece of backing material without using needles or looms. Anderson changed the name of his company to Interface Flooring Systems in 1982. The following year, Interface became a publicly traded corporation. Maintaining an emphasis on carpet tiles while expanding into other related product lines, Interface became by the late 1980s the fourth largest commercial carpet maker in the United States and the second-largest carpet tile maker in the world. Anderson also looked at how companies manufactured carpets and determined that they "were inherently unfriendly to the environment. Most carpet and carpet tiles are made from nylon refined from pools of petroleum; two known carcinogens, fiberglass and polyvinyl chloride (PVC) are chief components in carpet-backing materials; the dyes used to color carpets are flushed into the region's streams. When the carpet has outlived its usefulness, it generally is sent to landfills. By the late 1980s, virtually indestructible old carpets made up a growing part of the nation's waste." (Patton, "Interface, Inc.")

He led his company to policies of sustainable development which included reducing emissions and solid waste. Profitability increased, and recognition followed. His awards include the Millennium Award from Global Free, a position on Bill Clinton's President's Council on Sustainable Development, and the George and Cynthia Mitchell International Prize for Sustainable Development.

J&J

J & J Industries produces commercial broadloom carpets in Dalton. It is one of the largest companies of its kind. Exclusively a commercial carpet producer now, it once produced candy-striped carpets and braided rugs.

Rollins Jolly graduated from the University of Georgia and went to work in the textile mills of North Carolina and Georgia. He founded the Jolly Textiles and Dalton Cone company to sell "yarn, jute and duck backing, and yarn cones" and "to reprocess used cones and transform carpet remnants into rugs." His partner, Tom Jones graduated with a degree in industrial management from the Georgia Institute of Technology. They renamed the company J & J Industries. Later, the company started

DALTON Georgia
THE CARPET CAPITAL OF THE WORLD

using a process called "'fine gauge tufting' which used more needles per square inch to produce a very dense product. The unique product was much in demand and sold well." (Deaton, J & J Industries)

Today, the company sells primarily to airports, corporate offices, hospitals, retail stores, and schools. Also, "J & J has worked to be an industry leader in reducing pollutants and minimizing the environmental impact on air, water, and land. The nylon yarn and backing they use to make carpets are composed of some recycled materials, and post-consumer carpets are incorporated into cement, decking boards, and marine pilings (or plastic "plywood"). The company has also donated land adjacent to its facilities, which has been developed, in conjunction with such groups as the Nature Conservancy, into a wetlands area. These wetlands contain stormwater and establish a riparian habitat in the Conasauga River watershed." (Deaton, J & J Industries)

CARPET CAPITAL OF THE WORLD

Dalton is often referred to as the "Carpet Capital of the World," home to over 150 carpet plants. The industry employs more than 30,000 people in the Whitfield County area. More than 90% of the functional carpet produced in the world today is made within a 65-mile radius of the city.

It has moved from producing hand-tufted bedspreads to flooring for boardrooms, and looks for environmentally sound ways to keep doing so. In December 2019, carpet manufacturers hosted a sales representative meeting in Chattanooga, Tennessee (about thirty miles from Dalton). They discussed carpet, ceramic tile, hardwood floors, luxury vinyl tiles, and composite flooring, as more businesses and homeowners choose hard surfaces over carpet.

Manufacturing Success in Georgia

Above: Old Map of Southern States Railroads – Library of Congress

CHAPTER 5

MAJOR CHANGES IN THE NINETEENTH CENTURY:

Railroad Expansion, Ammunition and Firearms, Shoes, Civil War Textiles, Total War and an Emerging New South

During the War Between the States, Georgia "became an indispensable site for wartime manufacturing, combining a pre-war industrial base with extensive transportation linkages, and a geographic location secure for most of the war from the ravages of enemy armies." (Vanatta and Du)

The state produced munitions, firearms, uniforms, shoes, and materiel necessary for southern soldiers. Companies located in Columbus and Savannah even produced ironclad ships.

RAILROAD EXPANSION

Georgia's natural match was the transportation of manufactured products by rail. Rivers served as the original highways in Georgia, but river travel was dependent upon high and low water. The emerging railroad system, however, was not. It provided a faster and more reliable way for manufacturers to transport products to the market. Railroad development also spurred additional manufacturing. Vanatta and Du wrote

"Civil War Industry and Manufacturing" for the *New Georgia Encyclopedia.* The article states that "Railroad fever swept Georgia in the 1830s, and though track mileage was slow to develop, by 1860, the state controlled 1,420 of the South's 9,182 miles of track, second only to Virginia. Railroads spurred a host of associated industries, including iron foundries, rolling mills, and machine shops, all of which shaped and prepared iron, steel, and other metals for the many demands of the railroad business. These manufacturers also branched out to produce other metal goods; Macon's Findlay Iron Works, for example, built stationary steam engines for powering mills, cotton gins, and printing presses in the antebellum period. Railroads also effectively connected Georgia to the other states of the Confederacy, and by the beginning of the war, Georgia, and especially Atlanta, was the crucial nexus of Southern transportation and a heartland of southern industry." (Vanatta and Du)

Findlay Iron Works of Macon provides a *Manufacturing Success in Georgia* story: Born in Scotland, Robert Findlay helped establish Middle Georgia as an industry and transportation center in the 1800s. His legendary Scottish thrift allowed him to navigate the economic crisis of 1836-1859, and his vision allowed him to see manufacturing opportunities in southern industry, railroads, and in the ancient highways we know as rivers.

Schofield Iron Works, in Macon, made war materiel also. Founded in 1859

Then and Now:

In 1860, Georgia had around 1,500 miles of rails. Today, through mergers, Georgia's railroads are part of the Norfolk Southern subsidiary which operates almost 20,000 miles of railroad track in the United States.

Manufacturing Success in Georgia

"Schofield's Iron Works" from The Atlanta Constitution published May 16, 1880, says:

This famous institution was established in 1854, twenty-six years ago, and hence is no new candidate for public favor. During those years, with possibly a slight interruption, the founder has been constantly improving his vast machinery, and stocking the works with the finest and best patterns obtainable for the perfection of the work turned out. The present building located on the corner of Poplar and Fifth streets and adjoining passenger depot was built in 1859, but the constant annual increase of business has necessitated many additions. It is now conceded to be one of the few complete manufacturing establishments of the south.

The visitor, on beholding the scrupulous cleanliness of the shop, the excellent care of the machinery, which is all-new and of the most approved make, at once discovers the secret of success which has given the works their reputation for turning out and supplying the best machinery in the state. The same care and attention bestowed upon his own labor-saving machinery is given to work issued from the works, and hence, satisfaction is always the basis and result of every purchase and order. No work from east, west, north, or south excels that turned out by Schofield.

The Schofield Cotton Press, patented in 1867 by J.S. Schofield, the founder of these extensive works, is familiarly and favorably known in each county of each of the cotton states, and as an evidence of their worth and popularity, he guarantees that more of the Schofield presses are in use to-day than all of those of other builders aggregated.

Steam Engine and Boiler building are specialties with the proprietor, and on them, much personal attention is bestowed. Steam engines, both portable and stationary, with all the improvements in boiler and machinery of such sizes and styles as are best adapted to the use of planters for ginning or threshing purposes, and also for running light or heavy sawmills. Besides these specialties, Mr. Schofield builds sawmills of different kinds and sizes, to which he invites special examination. He can also supply grist mills, gin gearing, and is always prepared to supply all kinds of mill machinery and castings, both in iron or brass. His pattern-shop is also an important feature, embracing every variety of patterns, and to which daily additions are made by the pattern makers.

The prices for all his numerous manufacturers range low – at figures that cannot fail to give the utmost satisfaction. Correspondence is invited from all in want of anything in the machinery line, or if parties when in the city should visit his works, a personal inspection is earnestly solicited.

Mr. Schofield can supply all parties with as perfect machinery as can be obtained elsewhere.

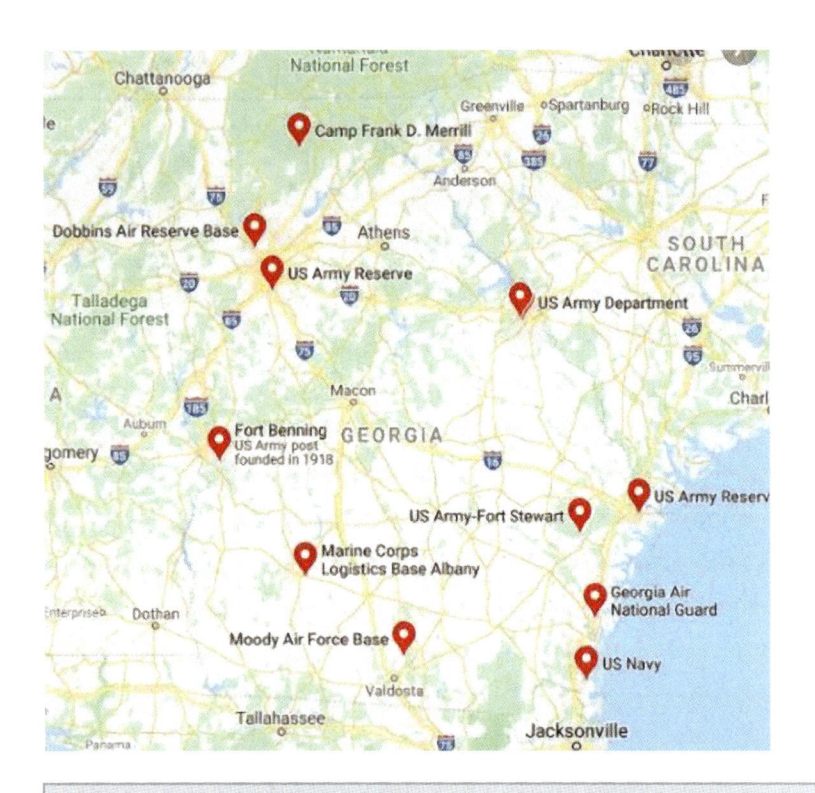

it grew into Taylor Iron Works. J.H. DuBose used the buildings from 1904-1912, followed by Adams Manufacturing from 1912-1940. Other owners included C.W. Farmer from 1942-1979 and L&M Manufacturers until 1995. NewTown Macon then listed the property as historic and endangered, and it was repurposed. Only a few of the original buildings remain.

AMMUNITION AND FIREARMS

At the beginning of the Civil War, the South realized that it was necessary to produce gunpowder: "Erected in a mere

---

Then and Now: Georgia's Strategic Geographic Location

Bordered by the Atlantic Ocean, the Appalachian Mountains, rivers, and the great Okefenokee Swamp, Georgia's geography provides a natural defense. Even the density of her vegetation augments this. Early Natives said that they'd rather fight from a cane break (an area overgrown with reeds like river cane) than from a fort. During the War for Independence, British soldiers called the wilderness around Augusta "The Hornet's Nest", complaining that there were rebels behind each tree and rock. By the time of the War Between the States, "Georgia's prime geographic location made the state an ideal center for wartime munitions production; it was distant from the fighting fronts, and its extensive rail network allowed powder to be quickly moved wherever it was needed." (Vanatta and Du)

The twentieth century saw a growth in military bases, too. Georgia has thirteen:

- Moody Air Force Base in Lanier and Lowndes Counties,
- Robins Air Force Base in Houston County,
- Dobbins Air Reserve Base in Cobb County,
- Fort Benning Army Base in Muskogee County,
- Fort Gillem Army Base in Clayton County,
- Fort Gordon Army Base in Richmond County,
- Fort McPherson Army Base in Fulton County,
- Fort Stewart Army Base in Liberty County,
- Hunter Army Airfield Army Base in Chatham County,
- Camp Frank D Merrill Army Base in Lumpkin County,
- Marine Corps Logistics Base at Albany Army Base in Dougherty County,
- Naval Air Station Atlanta Navy Base in Cobb County, and
- Kings Bay Submarine Navy Base in Camden County.

Looking forward, Georgia's new SpacePort is planned for Camden County, so Georgia exemplifies "Location, location, location."

Manufacturing Success in Georgia

Then and Now: Daniel Defense

Faith, Freedom, and Firearms are core beliefs on which Marty and Cindy Daniel built Daniel Defense. Georgia's geographic location on the southeastern coast of the United States made her a strategic defense point from day one. It's logical, then, that Metro Savannah is filled with historic forts and battlements.

It's also logical that a multimillion-dollar company based its operations in nearby Pooler, which is also home to the National Museum of the Mighty Eighth Air Force. Georgia knows defense. Daniel Defense's two hammer forges "are capable of pummeling out 70 tons of pressure to hammer-forged barrels at a rate of 4,000 strikes per four-minute cycle." (Landers)

Sales at Daniel Defense grew from $32,000 in 2012 to $32 million in 2020, and the company is "considered by many to be one of the top firearms manufacturers in the world today." (Landers)

Similar to the success stories of many industrial giants, Daniel Defense's story starts with failure. Marty Daniel "flunked out of the engineering program at Georgia Southern University— twice." (Daniel Defense / Company History).

A wise person once said that "A students become teachers, and B students end up working for the C students." There's truth here. C students are those who tried, failed, and tried again. They are the innovators. One study calls them the entrepreneurs, for one must learn what does not work to find what does. Here's the rest of the story: Marty's "turning point prompted a new approach to life and business: one of total domination. It would not be enough to simply go back to school and graduate; Marty needed to excel and dominate. He did so by making the Dean's List and, in 1985, graduating with an electrical engineering degree from the same university that sent him packing. Today, Marty sits on Georgia Southern Engineering School's Board of Advisors. In 2014 he worked with Governor Nathan Deal to establish the school's Manufacturing Engineering Degree Program," and "Daniel Defense was recognized by Inc. Magazine as one of the fastest-growing private companies in the United States for three consecutive years (2012, 2013, 2014). This prestigious recognition came at a time when the company experienced 1000% growth over a 10-year period."

Left: Wesley (Left) and Jason Moss (Right) show a couple of their Daniel Defense firearms. "We love to shoot and we love the quality of these guns that are manufactured in Georgia".

A Story of a Georgia Shoemaker

In June of 1992, Dianne Dent Wilcox, co-author of Manufacturing Success in Georgia, visited Mr. Joe and Mrs. Frances Etheridge, at their Griswoldville home, to collect their story for her history column Along the Garrison Road for The Jones County News. Wilcox learned that Joe Etheridge was the great-grandson of Aaron Stripling, a shoemaker at the famous Griswoldville Pistol Factory. This article ran on July 16th.

The stone said, "Aaron Stripling – Shoemaker," Mr. Ethridge explained: "I made that thing (the tombstone) and put it up there a few years ago. That was my great granddaddy and it's on his old homeplace, part of the rock quarry out there. You know, just below that sign, Rivers and Knox Quarry – just below there (now Martin Marietta Aggregates on Pitts Chapel Road). You cain't hardly tell where the old home house was. The road used to come in another way. That used to be the old plantation road.

"People have been through there in T-models. I remember T-model cars going through there. It was an old wagon road. That's all they had back there.

"Samuel Griswold built his foundry when my great-granddaddy was eight or nine or ten, maybe, and my great-granddaddy, he wouldn't fight in the War (Between the States). He was a shoemaker and tried to tell people that we needed a Union – united together – the North and the South.

"It was foolish to fight. We didn't have anything down here, industry, and such as the Northern people had. A lot of the homefolk criticized him but he wouldn't fight with them. But he made boots and supplied all the soldiers of this community which was a lot of them.

"When the Yankees came through, my great-granddaddy had a supply of leather buried under his shop. But my great-granddaddy, he left and went down in Twiggs County and spent the night with a widow down there, the first night, after the Yankees went on through here, he went back home. And two steers come back up out of that swamp that he thought was gone since they (the Federal soldiers and the scavengers or bummers who followed them) killed everything. Grandpa said that he never will forget that they were up there after his white pet hog and he remembered them catching that hog and killing it. They cooked him in the syrup kettle out there."

Later in the interview, Mr. Etheridge added, "Now, you have grown up since the war can have no idea how important it was to have a shoemaker in the neighborhood. You couldn't go to the stores and buy shoes. The people had to save all the hides from cows, horses, sheep, goats, dogs, and every other animal and either tan them into leather themselves" or carry them to a shoemaker. "Grandfather (Samuel Griswold) had a good many workers to shoe and leather was hard to get. He got sufficient upper leather and saw out the soles from wood and had them made by Aaron Stripling. The workers thought it would not do and complained about them but the old gentleman put a pair of them on himself. After this, there was no complaint and the wooden bottomed shoes were all right when they became used to them. I wish I could've wrote down all that stuff about things that happened back then."

---

eight months, the Confederate Powder Works comprised a two-mile-long series of castellated Gothic revival buildings, straddling the Augusta Canal, that were designed to efficiently convert sulfur, niter, and charcoal into finished powder. At peak production, the Confederate Powder Works was capable of producing as much as 6,000 pounds of gunpowder per day, and by the end of the war, more than 3 million pounds had been produced." (Vanatta and Du)

THIS WAS A START

Georgia still needed manufactured firearms, ammunition, uniforms, blankets, knapsacks, saddles, and shoes for her soldiers: "Arms and armament production, therefore, were also necessary for the Confederate war effort, and in Georgia, these tasks were undertaken by a mix of public and private industry spread among the state's larger urban centers." (Vanatta and Du)

The Atlanta Ironworks produced percussion caps, ammunition, and other materiel. Atlanta Machine Works manufactured forges for rifle works, and Georgia Railroad's machine shops made small cannons. The Columbus arsenal produced small-arms ammunition, and the Columbus Naval Iron Works made cannons and boilers for gunboats.

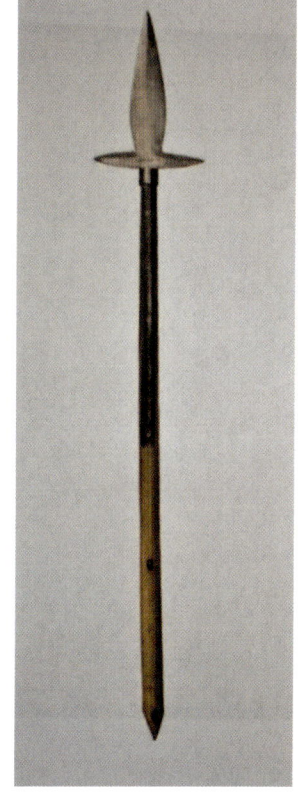

Above left: A rifled parrot gun stands guard at Chickamauga & Chattanooga National Military Park's Fort Oglethorpe Visitor's Center.

Above: A Griswoldville Pike is a long pole with an iron forged point used in hand to hand warfare.

Left: A historic marker at Griswoldville Battlefield tells how Federal soldiers targeted Griswoldville, Georgia, on their March to Sea to stop the production of pistols and pikes.

CHAPTER 5

43

Above: Sherman's troops rampaged through Georgia in what they called Total War. Federal soldiers who previously held jobs in manufacturing used their skills to help destroy Georgia's ability to transport products and personnel. They often heated and bent the railroad rails to prevent quick repair. Georgians called these twisted rails "Sherman's Neckties." Stone Mountain, Georgia, features one in their downtown historic area.

The Savannah arsenal moved to Macon and produced Parrott rifled cannons. Macon also produced pikes which were infantry weapons with pointed steel or iron heads on long wooden shafts, and short swords. Dalton made swords, Rome made cannons, Griswoldville made pikes and revolvers, and Athens produced bayonets and rifles.

CIVIL WAR TEXTILES

Another natural match was the cotton culture and the development of a textile industry because soldiers needed more than weapons: "Thirty-three mills were in operation on the eve of the war, producing the highest volume of textiles of any Southern state. At their peak during the war, these mills turned out more than 500,000 yards of cloth per week. Georgia's textile mills took up the task of producing cloth for uniforms, blankets, tents, and other uses, while the state's 125 boot and shoe manufacturers turned out their wares as quickly as possible to keep the Confederate armies marching." (Vanatta and Du)

Supplies and laborers were difficult to find. Women, slaves, and eventually prisoners helped fill the shortages. Manufacturers also faced shortages of raw materials: "By 1863 the Confederate

Manufacturing Success in Georgia

government had virtually monopolized the wool supply, forcing factories to produce only for government orders and leaving the civilian population with little access to woolen goods. Representing a broader trend, the Quartermaster Department's persistent purchases (or impressments) of the bulk of the state's textile and shoe manufacturers left civilians facing intense scarcity and exorbitant prices. These conditions often led to accusations of profiteering, pressuring the Georgia legislature to pass a Monopoly and Extortion Bill as early as December 1861." (Vanatta and Du)

TOTAL WAR

As a war that many expected to be completed quickly moved into its fourth year, General William Tecumseh Sherman declared total warfare in Georgia. If he and his men could stop the production and delivery of supplies, he reasoned, they could end the conflict: "The railroads that connected Georgia's industry to the rest of the Confederacy were a primary target for Sherman's forces, who followed the tracks from Tennessee to Savannah, ripping up rail as they went. Atlanta's factories were destroyed, and much of the city was burned. Cities like Augusta and Macon were spared, but without the rail connections through Atlanta, the products of their factories faced increasing difficulty in reaching the remaining Confederate forces." (Vanatta and Du)

THE NEW SOUTH

The end of the War Between the States "did not presage the decline of Georgia's industry; in fact, the roots of Georgia's New South efforts can be distinctly traced to the state's manufacturing experiences during the Civil War. The stimulus of war expanded industry across the state, such that between 1860 and 1870 the number of establishments increased from 1,890 to 3,836, and the value of yearly product nearly doubled, from $16.9 million to $31.1 million. Atlanta, once rebuilt, surged into the postbellum period intent on forging a new identity, one less reliant on northern manufacturers and more capable of producing needed goods at home. Industry continued to blossom across the state, and though cotton production still dominated, a more balanced economy emerged in the wake of Southern defeat." (Vanatta and Du)

CHAPTER 6

FOOD INDUSTRIES: COLA, PECANS, PEANUTS, ONIONS, CHICKENS

Pilgrim's Pride, Fieldale Farms, Crider Foods, Cagle's, Chick-fil-A, and Colas

Agribusiness is big business in Georgia, and adds approximately $73 billion to the economy annually. It involves ongoing research, knowledge and responsible use of chemicals, soil conservation, protection of the environment, distribution, manufacturing support, marketing, and may even produce biofuels. Newer crops in Georgia include blueberries, olives, and carrots, but the state is noted for its pecans, peanuts, onions, chickens, and two companies that help fuel the busy lives of Georgia's people: fast food and colas.

PECANS

The state of Georgia leads the nation in pecan production. Hurricane Michael threatened that status in 2018, but farmers worked to regain the position. No one in

Georgia is overly concerned whether you pronounce pecan as "pea can" or "pea con," and yes, they are grown in orchards on trees: "Pecans are a good source of protein and are loaded with essential vitamins and minerals, including iron, calcium and the B vitamins." (Georgia Grown Pecans)

Albany, in Dougherty County which claims to have six hundred thousand pecan trees, is known as the "Pecan Capital of the World", but orchards grow throughout the state. Georgia's commercial production of pecans began in 1901. Production reached forty million pounds by 1948. The crop is native, and used for holiday baking and in year-round cooking. Georgia now grows about one-third of all pecans in the United States with an average crop of eighty-eight million pounds each fall. The crop, harvested in October and November, is significant to Georgia: "In 1995, Georgia pecan wood was selected by the Atlanta Committee for the Olympic Games to make the handles of the torches for the 1996 Summer Olympic Games. These pecan-wood made torches were carried in the relays which took the torches from Athens, Greece, to the United States, then all around the country, culminating with the lighting of the Olympic flame in Atlanta on July 19, 1996." (Jones)

In 2018, disaster struck in the form of Hurricane Michael. Richard Nutt, a longtime pecan grower in Pitts, Georgia, said, "Michael harvested my entire crop, but with 100 miles per hour winds, I just don't know where they're harvested." Brad Haire, writing for *Farm Progress* said, "The mega storm's path mowed over the pecan-producing hub of the country's top pecan-producing state with 100-mph winds as harvest for the year's crop was getting underway, knocking nuts, limbs, and trees to the ground." Estimates made by the University of Georgia state that the storm cost farmers "50 percent of the state's crop, $100 million in lost income, and about three-quarters of a million individual trees." (Haire)

The bright side is that now younger trees have more sunlight in which to develop. Richard Nutt also said, "We've had losses before. We just go back to the field and start again." Fortuitously, his farm operation is diversified and generational. Son-in-law, Dennis Stone,

Above: From the Rhodes family farm in Pineview, Georgia

CHAPTER 6

Above: One of Georgia's seasonal traditions involves digging peanuts directly from the field where they grow, and boiling them to eat as snacks. Most convenience stores and farmer's markets sell salted and Cajun seasoned boiled peanuts year-round.

and grandson Shane Rhodes will nurture pecan production while they continue to harvest cotton, melons, peanuts, and chickens.

PEANUTS

According to the University of Georgia's Extension Center website, "Georgia is the number one producer of peanuts in the United States, and Georgia peanut farmers provide more than 45 percent of the U.S. peanut crop each year. Georgia peanuts produce a farm gate value (market value minus selling cost) of well over $600 million." Peanuts grow beneath the surface and do well in the sandy soil of South Georgia, which leads the nation in production with "approximately 49 percent of the crop's national acreage and production. In 2014 Georgia farmers harvested 591,000 acres of peanuts, the official state crop, for a yield of 2.4 billion pounds." (Beasley)

The Georgia Farm Bureau reports that "The state's peanut growers are planting an estimated 600,000 acres in 2019, down 10% from 2018, when they planted 665,000 acres."

Peanut plants are not native to the United States: "Brought to the South by explorers from South America via Africa, the peanut is thought to have been grown in Georgia about a decade before the Civil War (1861-65). Despite its name, the peanut is not a true nut but a member of the legume family." (Beasley)

Peanuts require a 150-day growing season and sandy soil. Georgia's coastal plain, south of the fall line, provides the perfect environment. After World War II, the growing area included about one million Georgia acres. In 2005, peanut acreage was approximately 755,000. The peanut industry involves the "grower, buyer, sheller, manufacturer, and such allied industries as storage and transportation." (Beasley)

The Georgia Farm Bureau reports that scientific research conducted by the University of Georgia and the U.S. Department of Agriculture "has resulted in dramatically improved yield and quality. Some of the state's critical advancements include improved varieties, better harvest techniques, water management through irrigation, improved pest management, and

Manufacturing Success in Georgia

such new technologies as yield monitors, variable rate application of fertilizers, and irrigation water. The University of Georgia's food scientist research has improved the quality, nutrition, and marketability of peanuts. Research in the areas of policy and marketing have given peanut producers around the county better opportunities for competing in a global market." (Beasley)

Georgia born peanut expert Dr. J. Ernest Harvey, Jr. (1935-2020) traveled the world helping countries develop peanut crops to better feed their people and to provide economic development in their homelands. A graduate of both Abraham Baldwin Agricultural College and the University of Georgia, he spoke at conferences worldwide. One of those conferences was in Las Vegas. Dr. Harvey said he stepped onto a hotel elevator that had an attendant. The attendant asked, "When do you think all these farmers will leave?"

Dr. Harvey, who had just given the keynote address in a business suit that did not identify him as a farmer said, "I don't know, why do you ask?"

The young attendant replied, "Well, they all come to Vegas with a one-hundred-dollar bill in one hand and the Ten Commandments in the other. They haven't broken either one, yet."

If you love PayDay candy bars, this Georgian designed a long shelf life peanut used in the recipe for years. Georgia lost him to COVID-19 in July 2020.

Wilcox County, Georgia, peanut grower Jerry Rhodes, his son Dennis, and grandsons Jackson and Jeremy get text messages to their cell phones when a peanut irrigation cycle is complete or needs attention. They rely on the use of global technology such as satellite aligned planting rows in their fields. In addition to peanuts, the Rhodes family grows cotton and corn.

OLIVER FARM ARTISAN OILS

A new industry of producing pecan and other specialty oils will impact future markets. Clay and Valerie Oliver of Pitts, Georgia, started their business by exploring alternative fuel sources.

Clay says, "I began researching, visiting oil plants, and talking to individuals in this field. My initial thought was to make my own fuel. The equipment needed to extract oil is expensive, and the savings on fuel would not pay for the equipment for many years. I was fortunate enough to meet a couple of people who influenced me to consider growing, processing, and selling food-grade oil. During this time, I discovered the cold-pressed method of oil extraction which does not use chemicals or high temperatures to remove the oil. This process leaves valuable vitamins and nutrients in the oil. The oil also retains its natural flavor and color." (Oliver Farm)

The family grew its first crop of sunflowers in 2012, and began cold

Right: Vidalia Onions in the Field Almost Ready for Harvest

Below: Sweet Vidalia Onions Ready for the Table

pressing oil from pecans and peanuts grown in their home county. Their oils "can be used in fuel, cleaners, soap, cosmetic products, and have medicinal uses as well." (Oliver Farm)

Oliver Farm sells sunflower, pecan, green peanut, benne, okra, pumpkin seed, nigella seed, coriander seed, poppy seed oils, and hosts farm tours.

ONIONS

Occasionally, agriculture and manufacturing meet in more ways than the production of farm equipment to grow and transport produce. The idea to provide an East Coast option to California produce, thereby reducing transportation costs, increasing quality, ensuring fresher food, and boosting local economies means that if Georgia grows produce, our East Coast food is fresher. A more practical consideration for investors is that "Farm returns are good when equity returns aren't." (Newkirk)

Historic manufacturers who saw this potential include automobile magnate Henry Ford and technology wizard Bill Gates. Ford conducted agricultural experiments at Richmond Hill and Gates ventured briefly into Vidalia onions.

Vidalia onions are special: "By federal law, the squat, sweet-flavored Vidalia onion can be grown and packaged in only one region in Georgia." (Newkirk)

According to *Vidalia Onions*, "All Vidalias are sweet onions, but not all sweet onions are Vidalias." A Vidalia onion "has a unique flat shape, is grown from a yellow onion granex seed variety, which is tested for a minimum of three years to ensure it meets proper standards, has a produce identification sticker with a PLU code of 4159 in grocery stores, and is grown in one of 20 South Georgia counties outlined by the Federal Marketing Order No. 955." (*Vidalia Onions*)

Accidentally discovered in the 1930s, the once seasonal treat is available year-round per the adoption of refrigerated warehouses, and "Vidalia farmers, many with corporate pedigrees and most with international experience, have parlayed their onions into a $100 million to $168 million annual market." Today, "approximately 200 million pounds of Vidalia onions are distributed across the country and Canada each year. Vidalia onions are the Official State Vegetable of Georgia. (Newkirk)

CHICKENS

Georgia is a world leader in producing chicken and egg products. Companies include "Gold Kist, Fieldale Farms, Claxton, Mar-Jac and Cagle's" who handle "raw materials, processing, and distribution." (Weinberg)

Georgia estimates the economic impact of poultry production (to include turkeys) at $28 billion annually. The USA Poultry and Egg Council Export headquarters is located in Stone Mountain, Georgia. Farm women produced and sold eggs before World War I, and rail transport accelerated the poultry market by 1924. In the 1930s, north Georgian Jesse Jewell offered farmers chicks and feed on credit, then began his processing plant and hatchery. By the time of World War II, the War Food Administration "reserved all

CHAPTER 6

the processed chicken in North Georgia" which only built the industry (Weinberg). Then the health-conscious public raised the stakes again in the latter part of the twentieth century, and "by 1995 Georgia annually processed more than 5 billion pounds of chicken" (Weinberg). Side industries, such as fertilizer processing plants, grew with poultry processing and egg production. The industry, started in north Georgia is now moving south, across the state, as cooling technology for chicken houses advances.

PILGRIM'S PRIDE

Pilgrim's Pride is a leading global poultry and prepared foods company. Although it is Brazilian owned, it is based in Colorado. It has thirty-six production facilities and sixteen prepared foods facilities across the U.S., Puerto Rico, Mexico, the United Kingdom. and Continental Europe, and maintains business hubs in Ambrose, Athens, Bowdon, Bremen, Canton, Carrollton, Commerce, Douglas, Elberton, Ellijay, Gainesville, Talking Rock, and Talmo, Georgia. Pilgrim's can process 45.2 million birds per week and produces 13.3 billion pounds of live chicken annually. (Pilgrim's: A Global Story)

FIELDALE FARMS

Fieldale Farms, another major Georgia poultry producer, operates in Baldwin, Cornelia, Eastanollee, Gainesville, and Murrayville, Georgia. It offers natural whole birds, cut-up, skinless, and boneless chicken parts, and fully-cooked products. Fieldale operates with the latest equipment and technology and keeps in mind the health of its consumers.

CRIDER FOODS

Crider Foods, located in Stillmore, Georgia, is a global food manufacturer and one of the world's largest canning and fully cooked chicken companies. They "run can sizes from 3 ounces to 96 ounces and produce for leading food brands as well as private label accounts, club stores, and the foodservice industry." (Crider Foods)

Located in Emanuel County, the company offers much-needed jobs for residents of rural southeast Georgia.

CAGLE

Cagle's, one of the top global *poultry* producers, grew from a one-man operation, selling live birds and then processing them while the customer waited in the Five Points area of downtown Atlanta. The family-owned company has sold "more than 400 million pounds of chicken to supermarkets, food distributors, food-processing companies, fast-food chains, restaurants, and schools since the 1940s." Because of the massive production of poultry products, Georgia has been declared the "Poultry Capital of the World": "By 2006, the industry directly employed more than 51,000 Georgians, with another 50,000 state residents working indirectly for the industry – at the University of Georgia, the Georgia Institute of Technology, pharmaceutical companies, equipment suppliers, and country agricultural extension offices." (Weinberg)

A January 27, 2015 article for *Atlanta Magazine* lists further statistics: Poultry constitutes 47% of Georgia's state agriculture business, people in the US consume an average of 21 dozen eggs annually, chicken overtook beef as America's favorite meal in 1991, and Georgia produces 2.4 million metric tons of broilers each year for an annual economic impact of $38 billion. The United States Department of Agriculture (USDA) reports that in 2018, Georgia produced 8,168,400 pounds of broiler chicken with a production value of $4,566,136, and Georgia produced 1,360,300,000 broilers according to the USDA's "2019 State Agriculture Overview." The department reports 4,871.1 million eggs produced, too. Contract farmer Wes Hopper says, "Chickens have been very good to our family."

CHICK-FIL-A

Truett Cathy and his brother Ben established The Dwarf Grill in Hapeville in 1946. They built it near a Ford auto plant with the idea of bringing in its hungry employees. It worked. Their website says that in 2019 the company "has the highest same-store sales and is the largest quick-service chicken restaurant chain in the United States based on annual system-wide sales." An advertising campaign once claimed that Chick-fil-A didn't invent the chicken, just the chicken sandwich. The company, not open on Sunday to respect the religious choices of its employees, continues to grow in 2020. Chick-fil-A not only grows its business, but it grows its people. That's about seventy people per restaurant. The website goes on to say that "Truett Cathy had a special place in his heart for his employees. He believed that giving people the opportunities they need to succeed helps all of us prosper. Truett never went to college himself. That's why since 1973, Chick-fil-A has given more than $35 million in college scholarships to Chick-fil-A restaurant team members wishing to pursue higher education." The company now operates in forty-seven states, and Washington,

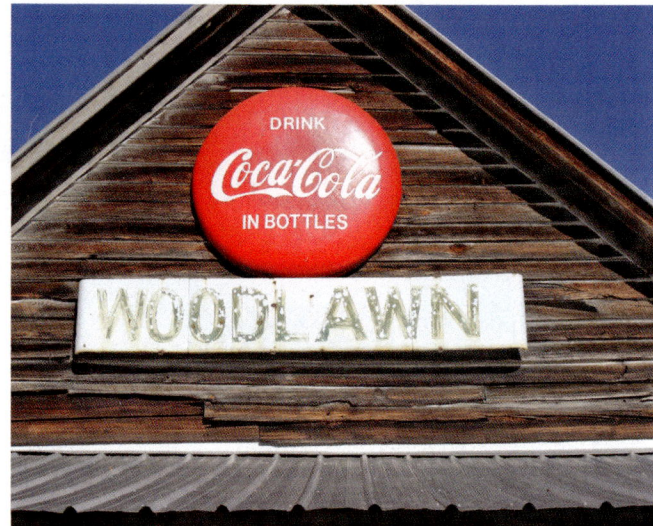

Above: One of Georgia's many painted Coca-Cola ads still shows its original colors in Pitts, Georgia.

Right: Vintage 6 ½ ounce contour side glass Coca-Cola bottle.

Above: An early advertisement

D.C., and looks for further opportunities. Its training program even helps young entrepreneurs acquire their own franchises. While other restaurant employees might say "Thank you, and come again" to customers, Chick-fil-A employees say, "It was my pleasure to serve you." Alicia Kelso of *Forbes* writes that "Chick-fil-A is on a staggering growth course to become the third-largest quick-service restaurant in the county." The article shows that in 2017, Chick-fil-A's average sales at $4.4 million exceeds McDonald's by $2 million and KFC by $3.3 million per restaurant. *Franchise Times* says that "total company revenue was $3.8 billion in 2019 compared to $3.0 billion in 2018, an increase of 26.7 percent" (Hamburger). Net earnings for Chick-Fil-A "were $670.1 million in 2019 versus $434 million in 2018, an increase of 54.2 percent." (Hamburger)

Two other interesting tidbits come from the Chick-fil-A website: "By the end of 2019, every Chick-fil-A across the country will serve chicken raised without antibiotics," and the "Chick-fil-A Foundation awarded $1.23 million to 23 not-for-profit organizations across 13 states through the True Inspiration Awards and $14.5 million in scholarships in 2018 to restaurant Team Members nationwide." (Kelso)

Of course, few people enjoy a chicken sandwich without a great cola.

Manufacturing Success in Georgia

Left: The Coca-Cola bottling plant in Helena-McRae has operated for over a hundred years.

COCA-COLA

Dr. John S. Pemberton, also a pharmacist, was born in Crawford County, Georgia, and created a soft drink that could be sold at drug store soda fountains, that changed the world: "Pemberton was a veteran Confederate lieutenant colonel who served on the first Georgia pharmacy licensing board after the war. His state-of-the-art laboratory for chemical analysis and manufacturing became the first state-run facility to conduct tests of soil and crop chemicals." (Cooksey)

To create his new soft drink, Pemberton mixed the flavored syrup with carbonated water at his Atlanta pharmacy, and his bookkeeper, Frank M. Robinson said, "Call it Coca-Cola." They charged five cents per glass, and in the first year, "sales averaged a modest nine servings per day in Atlanta. Today, daily servings of Coca-Cola beverages are estimated at 1.9 billion globally. Mississippi businessman Joseph Biedenham moved the fountain drink to bottles, and Benjamin Thomas, Joseph Whitehead, and John Lupton developed what became the Coca-Cola worldwide bottling system." (Coca-Cola History)

Drinking sodas soon became synonymous with a growing teenage culture and drug store soda fountains, serving soft drinks, ice cream, and sandwiches flourished. Soda makers often imitated the taste and marketing of another company's product. To combat this, Coca-Cola designed and produced its distinctive contoured bottles in 1916, although they did not trademark the unique design until 1977. Marketing efforts began with coupons, newspaper advertisements, and the production of promotional items bearing the Coca-Cola logo. Examples of advertising highlight displays at Atlanta's famous World of Coke museum. Today, Coca-Cola products include variants on the main brand like Vanilla Coke and Cherry Coke, low or no sugar versions, Dasani bottled water, Minute Maid juice products, and POWERADE sports drinks.

Marketing Week, published in Great Britain, reported on July 16, 2018, that Diet Coke sales exceeded Classic Coca-Cola as sugar taxes and a more health-conscious consumer shifted the market: "The figures are a positive sign for Coca-Cola, proving that heavy investment into its low-sugar variants has, at least initially, paid off." (Fleming)

Above: Royal Crown Bottle Photos courtesy of Renee Ball Hughes

CHAPTER 6

Right: Royal Crown Bottle Photos courtesy of Renee Ball Hughes

Coca-Cola has bottling plants in Athens, Atlanta, Augusta, Bainbridge, Brunswick, Columbus, Dublin, Jasper, Lawrenceville, Macon, Marietta, Rome, Sandy Springs, Savannah, Statesboro, Sylvester, Valdosta, and West Point, Georgia. The fizz first heard in Atlanta now makes a splash worldwide. The World of Coke in Atlanta attracts people from across the globe. Over twenty-three million people have walked through the doors and sampled one hundred products or more.

ROYAL CROWN

In 1905, a "young pharmacist named Claud Hatcher developed…a bottled drink to sell in his family's grocery store" and Royal Crown, Chero-Cola, and Nehi were born at Union Bottling Works (Bowers "Royal Crown"). RC reached nationwide distribution but never achieved the popularity of brands like Coca-Cola or Pepsi.

In 1954, Royal Crown "became the first beverage company to nationally distribute soft drinks in cans." (Bowers)

Other firsts included the production of "the first low-calorie diet cola (Diet Rite), the first caffeine-free diet cola (RC 100), and the first diet cherry cola (Diet Cherry RC)." (Bowers)

Cadbury Schweppes of Great Britain bought RC Cola in October 2000.

Manufacturing Success in Georgia

Left: Model T at Atlanta's Swan House

CHAPTER 7

The Transportation Industry:

Georgia Ports Authority, Brunswick Auto Port, Ford, GM, KIA, Blue Bird, E-Z Go, Club Car, and Great Dane

GEORGIA PORTS AUTHORITY AND BRUNSWICK AUTO PORT

Transportation in Georgia moved from foot traffic to riding horses (using horses, mules or oxen to pull wagons), traveling by water (pole boat, raft, or steamboat), riding the rails, to automobiles, trucks, ocean-bound supercarriers, and aircraft.

The Savannah Economic Development article "Port of Savannah: A Window to the World" says that "Savannah is home to the Port of Savannah, the largest single-terminal container facility of its kind in North America. Operated by the Georgia Ports Authority and specializing in breakbulk, containers, Roll-On / Roll-Off (for wheeled cargo that can be driven onto or off a ship), heavy-lift and project cargo. The port is comprised of two modern, deep-water terminals: Ocean Terminal and Garden City Terminal. The Port of Savannah is the fastest-growing and fourth-busiest port in the nation, with 36 weekly vessel calls, more than any other container terminal on the U.S. East Coast. In the fiscal year 2019, the Georgia Ports Authority moved a record 4.5 million 20-foot equivalent

Ships moving into and out of the Savannah Port

containers and more than 650,000 auto and machinery units."

Tyler H. Jones, for *The Brunswick News*, wrote in "Brunswick Auto Port Doubled Capacity in 2017" that "The facility moved more than 600,000 vehicles in the fiscal year 2017, and the Georgia Ports Authority hopes to see increased growth in the coming months, according to Griff Lynch, the authority's executive director, who spoke Thursday at the annual State of the Port luncheon on Jekyll Island. Colonel's Island, one of three Port of Brunswick facilities, is the second busiest auto port in the country, behind one in Baltimore, and is the nation's largest." The port has the capacity for 800,000 vehicles per year. A planned expansion will raise the number to 1.4 million.

In 2019, *Business Insider* writer Josie Mumm says Hartsfield-Jackson Airport handles close to 300,000 passengers a day, "sees 107 million passengers a year and, employs 63,000 people." It has 1.3 million square feet of cargo warehouses and twenty-eight parking spaces for cargo aircraft. A look back at the development of Georgia's transportation manufacturing shows why the seaports and airports need to handle such numbers.

Manufacturing Success in Georgia

FORD: MASS PRODUCTION AND BIOGRAPHICAL NOTES

Henry Ford, the United States' first billionaire, started his car manufacturing business in Detroit, Michigan; but through friendships and partnerships, soon had winter quarters in Florida, and Richmond Hill (then called Ways or Ways Station), Georgia. Although Henry Ford is often credited with the invention of mass production, he simply improved upon ideas brought to him by others. Ransom E. Olds (an innovator who built a steam car by 1897, and the namesake of Oldsmobile) had developed a mass assembly line by 1901.

Ford heard about the mass assembly idea from an employee who visited a Swift meatpacking plant in 1912. William Klann was invited to do a Swift meatpacking plant tour by his neighbor. Klann realized that these butchers were producing ten times the amount of packed beef than other companies. They had a process they called the dis-assembly line. One butcher made one cut and the next butcher made another. In performing the same task over and over, each person on the line became extremely proficient at it. They were able to outperform their competition ten to one. Klann took this idea back to his boss, Henry Ford. People give Henry Ford credit for the modern-day assembly line, but it was William Klann and the neighbor who invited him on a plant tour who introduced the idea to Ford. Several people were working with Ford who helped develop ideas. Ford's development team included William Klann, Peter E. Martin, Charles E. Sorensen, C. Howard Wills, Clarence C. Avery, Charles Ebender, Jozef Galamb, and Walter Flanders. By 1913, the company introduced the moving-chassis assembly line. Ford's assembly line improvements decreased the time it took to produce a Model T from 12.5 hours to 93 minutes by 1914.

Ford's first Model T's were constructed using a station-build approach in which a team of workers walked to the car. In April 1913, Ford began using a moving conveyor belt system to bring components to workers trained for individual tasks, and mass production was born. The implementation of this modern assembly line reduced the number of workers needed, reduced assembly time, and increased the number of automobiles built. Ford's production went from 19,050 in 1910 to 68,773 in 1912, and peaked at 2,011,125 in 1923. When the Model T went out of production in 1927, over fifteen million had been built. Ford met his dream of making cars affordable for everyone. In the beginning,

CHAPTER 7

The Ford complex buildings at Berry College include the English Gothic styled Clara Hall, Mary Hall, the Alumni Center, the Ford Gymnasium, Ford Auditorium, Ford Dining Hall, and the Admission Office.

Model T's cost between $825–$950. Mass production brought the prices down to between $360–$600.

Jason Moss used this illustration to begin the 2018 Georgia Manufacturing Summit and noted that "One opportunity, one new connection, or one new idea can change the world." Ford established a sales department in Atlanta by 1907. Next, he established the Ford Motor Company Assembly Plant in Atlanta, which operated from 1915 to 1942 making Model Ts, Model As, and V-8s. It combined assembly, sales, service, and administration to one location and sold a peak of 22,000 vehicles annually. When the United States War Department bought Ford's Ponce de Leon Avenue plant, Ford Motors opened a new plant in Hapeville. In 2008, Porsche purchased the Hapeville plant and used it as a test track.

Another major industrial advance Ford introduced was a wage change. Common wages for the time were $2.34 for a nine-hour day, and Ford announced it would pay $5 for an eight-hour day. One of Ford's considerations was that well-paid employees were also more likely to become customers, and Ford needed a more stable and well-trained workforce. Performing the same task for hours on an assembly line bored many employees, so the percentages of employees who quit forced continuous and expensive hiring. New employees, seeking the $5 a day wage, agreed to

Manufacturing Success in Georgia

meet company standards for sobriety, responsible home budget management, and a wholesome home environment to be assessed by the company. The policy reduced absenteeism and turnover while workers became more skilled at their tasks, and with more drivers, the suburbs and highway networks grew.

In the 1920s, Ford sought ways around a British monopoly on rubber and collaborated with his friend Harvey Firestone. Together with Thomas Edison, the friends experimented with several agricultural projects on an old plantation Ford bought called Richmond. Eventually, Ford and Firestone decided that synthetic products would replace rubber and the area of the old Richmond Plantation became Richmond Hill.

Henry Ford was an industrialist, and a philanthropist. Ford, in 1925, when he purchased property near Savannah, intended to give Georgians better employment opportunities. He established a sawmill at Ways Station which moved the timber industry forward. On his arrival in Bryan County, Ford immediately provided funds to local schools. He had only completed the sixth grade, strongly valued education, and understood its value in the workplace.

Ford and his wife, Clara Jane Bryant Ford also developed a special relationship with Berry College in Rome, Georgia. They visited the campus in 1923 after meeting its founder, Martha Berry, at a dinner hosted by Thomas Edison. A newspaper article titled "He Was Real Friendly" says that Ford donated money for buildings, specifically "the Ford Complex, West Mary Hall, East Mary Hall, and Clara Hall. Ford also funded the building of a reservoir, a gym, a dining hall, and an auditorium, among other structures that still stand today." The article discusses his lasting contribution as the work/study philosophy of Berry College: "Ford provided jobs so that students could work their way through higher education. He last visited Berry in March 1947." Hilda Mayo Crenshaw (1929-2020) remembered acting as chauffeur to Mr. and Mrs. Ford when they visited Berry. She was a student at the time, and one of the few women on campus who could drive. Mrs. Ford advocated women's suffrage, so she welcomed interactions with college women. Hilda Mayo Crenshaw enjoyed driving the Fords to various events.

In 1937, Ford hired one of Thomas Edison's chief chemists at Fort Myers, H.K. Ukkelberg, "to find new crops or better varieties of old crops grown in this section and to develop new uses for these crops and available waste materials." (Bryan)

They established a lab at Richmond Hill, extracting alcohol from rice and sweet potatoes, mixing it with gasoline, and using it for fuel. They reclaimed old rice fields for peas, carrots, mustard, turnips, beets, broccoli, rutabagas, onions, cabbage, Irish potatoes, okra, cucumbers, cotton, and other crops. They also experimented with oil-producing plants such as tung trees, perilla, chia, castor beans, and abutilon. Sweet potatoes, water chestnuts, and soybeans produced usable starches and slag conditioned soil. These agricultural

Above: Photos courtesy of Roberta Wallace Jolley

experiments proved less profitable than automobiles, but they show Ford as an innovator in several ventures.

Ford pursued similar projects in the north. By compressing wood waste from his sawmills and auto plants, he developed a charcoal briquette, first marketed using the name Ford, and now using Kingsford for Edward G. Kingsford who helped Ford procure timberland. In the twenty-first century, Kingsford processes a hundred million tons of wood waste into charcoal annually.

Although Georgians honored Ford in 1941 by changing the name Ways Station to Richmond Hill, Ford spent his time in Detroit supervising the production of aircraft, tanks, trucks, jeeps, and landing craft. The United States Infantry established anti-aircraft training at Camp Stewart on sections of Ford's property in Georgia. Unfortunately, Ford suffered a stroke in 1945. Henry Ford II took control of Ford Motor Company, and in Georgia, Camp Stewart became Fort Stewart, with Southern Kraft Timberland Corporation and International Paper Company purchasing the rest of Ford's Georgia holdings

Henry Ford's impact in the United States may never be fully measured. His cars made history and even though he did not produce the Mustang in Georgia, this 1966 Survivor shows that Georgians still love his cars. A Survivor is a show car in running condition and without any modifications from the manufacturer's specification.

GENERAL MOTORS

The Doraville Assembly Plant of General Motors operated from 1947 until 2008. General Motors also manufactured cars at Lakewood Assembly from 1927 until 1990. Models produced at Doraville include the 1947 Buick Super Woody, 1951 Oldsmobile 88, 1951 Buick Super 8 Special, 1953 Buick Skylark, 1955-1957 Buick Century, 1956 Oldsmobile Supper 88, 1957 Pontiac Star Chief, 1958 Pontiac Bonneville, 1960 Oldsmobile Super 88, 1965 Chevrolet Impala, 1972 Pontiac Catalina, 1976 Chevrolet Monte Carlo, 1988-1995 Oldsmobile Cutlass Supreme, 1982-1996 Oldsmobile Cutlass Ciera,

Manufacturing Success in Georgia

1997-2005 Chevrolet Venture, 1997-2005 Pontiac Trans Sport / Montana, 1997-2004 Oldsmobile Silhouette, 1997-1999 Opel Sintra, 2005-2007 Buick Terraza, 2005-2007 Saturn Relay, 2005-2009 Chevrolet Uplander, and the 2005-2009 Pontiac Montana SV6. Models produced at Lakewood include Chevrolets, Pontiacs, Oldsmobiles, GMC Trucks, and the Chevy Caprice.

But General Motors is not finished in Georgia. The *Atlanta Journal-Constitution* reported in 2013 that GM was hiring a thousand "software developers, database managers, and other high-skilled workers to design the company's back-office technical infrastructure" to work at a $26 million technology development center in Roswell." (Bluestein)

A *Georgia Industries* site article, written by Ashley Varnum says that "Georgia is home to more than 300 automotive-related facilities, and the automotive industry contributes more than $3 billion to our economy. Thanks to our airport, seaports, and central location amid Southeastern OEMs (Original Equipment Manufacturers), we are ideally situated to move product to customers both domestically and internationally; and have the skilled workforce and resources needed for manufacturing. Georgia has been an established automotive manufacturing center since 1909 when the first automobile was assembled in the state. Throughout the past hundred years, leading automotive companies have consistently chosen Georgia as their home for manufacturing, assembly, headquarters, and innovation centers."

Then and Now

The Doraville General Motors plant is now a movie studio. In 2018, the film industry had a $9.5 million impact on the state's economy and was responsible for more than 92,000 jobs in the state.

CHAPTER 7

63

KIA

The South Korean company was founded in 1944 as Kyungsung Precision Industry – a maker of steel tubing and bicycle parts. It also made Korea's first indigenous bicycle – the Samchully in 1951. Kia Motors America got its start in 1992 and today is part of the Hyundai Motor Group. Its most popular model is the Kia Soul. In Georgia, Kia manufactures the Telluride, Sorento, and the Optima. According to Kia's website, their West Point, Georgia, facility is the only Kia manufacturing plant in the United States and the only automaker in Georgia. News anchor and columnist Patankar, calls Kia, "The world's 4th largest car manufacturer behind Volkswagen, Toyota, and General Motors."

In addition to manufacturing, Kia focuses on training. Their training center, in partnership with Georgia Quick Start, "houses robotics, welding, and electronics labs, classrooms, and equipment for training on state-of-the-art programmable logic controllers." (Kia. The Training Center)

Sands wrote *Kia Motors Celebrates Decade of Manufacturing in Georgia in 2019*. It says that Kia's West Point operation

> **Then and Now**
>
> In 2020, Kia (KMMG) shifted gears in production and manufactured over fifteen thousand medical shields (personal protection devices) for Georgia's Emergency Management Agency (GEMA). The shift "expands Kia's 'Accelerate the Good' efforts to help people impacted by the COVID-19 pandemic" and supplied Georgia's front-line health care workers (Kia). They plan to increase output to meet needs as they arise. Kia opened its doors in 2010, so their "Accelerate the Good" philanthropy in 2020 marks ten years of Georgia operations. KMMG continues to plan, educate, give, and grow in West Point and worldwide.

Manufacturing Success in Georgia

Left: *Blue Bird Bus*

"was the company's first manufacturing hub to open in North America. It has so far helped create more than fifteen thousand local jobs, and produced more than three million vehicles. The 2,200-acre site has played a key role in strengthening Kia's presence in the U.S. market ever since, and currently has a production capacity of 340,000 vehicles per year" with three thousand employees. The company philosophy focuses on trust, teamwork, and making today better than yesterday.

BLUE BIRD

The Blue Bird Corporation was founded by Albert L. Luce, Sr. in 1932 at Fort Valley, Georgia. Luce, a Ford dealer since 1925, was approached by a customer who wished to transport workers. To answer the inquiry, Luce developed a wooden body and placed it on a Model T. His "invention" did not last as long as anticipated, so Luce began using sheet metal and steel and focused on marketing school buses. His first became Blue Bird No. 1. Family controlled the company until 1990, and now it is publicly owned.

Blue Bird manufactures school buses, transit buses, mobile libraries, and mobile police command centers. In the late twentieth century, Blue Bird was the largest school bus manufacturer in the nation. They can produce seventy buses a day in

Now:

Luce Heart Institute at The Medical Center, Navicent Health in Macon, Georgia, is named for Albert L. "Buddy" Luce, Jr. Luce retired Blue Bird Corporation President and CEO. Luce, after receiving heart treatment at what was then the Medical Center of Central Georgia, contributed $3 million toward the construction of the Institute. The institute opened in 2008, and continues to treat thousands of patients from central and south Georgia.

the Fort Valley facility and employ 2,300 people.

Beginning in the 1990s, Blue Bird developed environmentally-friendly vehicles. These include alternative-fuel buses, propane school buses, gasoline operated school buses to replace diesels, and fully electric buses.

The first electric school buses were developed using a $4.4 million grant from the United States Department of Energy and other investors and rolled off the assembly line in September 2018. Fully electric buses can operate up to one hundred twenty miles without a recharge. Charging time for advanced models has been reduced to three hours from the previous eight. They are zero-emission vehicles. Blue Bird's website boasts that electric buses need:

- No Engine Oil Changes
- No Engine Air Filter Change
- No Smog Check/Testing
- No Spark or Glow Plug, or Coil Replacements
- No Transmission Maintenance
- Brake Pad Change Intervals are Longer
- Fewer Coolant Changes Needed.

Right: While hundreds of people could not work during the COVID-19 pandemic, truck drivers worked double shifts to maintain over the ground logistic operations. Johnny Fields drives for McLendon Enterprises, Inc. based in Toombs County and delivers supplies and equipment for highway and road construction, water and sewer systems including treatment plants, and site work for commercial buildings and residential areas in southeast Georgia. McLendon, established in 1979, is a full-service construction company with approximately one hundred sixty employees.

Then and Now: Thank you!

Logistics is the coordination of moving things from one place to another, and our truck drivers hold a special place in the hearts of Americans for moving things over the road. We once even called them "The White Knights" because they often helped stranded drivers on the highways.

In 2020, the supply chain was stretched to the breaking point during the first announcement of the COVID-19 pandemic. Who would have thought that the availability of toilet paper would be a leading indicator of the crisis? The entire logistics industry and end to end supply chain were impacted. Essential workers were allowed to keep working as the nation faced quarantines and shut downs, and Americans gained a new appreciation for the great men and women who drive the truck that delivers almost everything we consume. Thank you.

Manufacturing Success in Georgia

Then and Now

In 1932, Bobby Jones and Clifford Roberts founded The Augusta National Golf Club, and the Master's Tournament has been played here since 1934. It's the natural place for golf cart production. Yamaha Motor Manufacturing Corporation of America was founded in 1986. They also produce golf carts in Georgia along with "motorcycles, scooters, all-terrain vehicles and side-by-side vehicles, snowmobiles, outboard motors, personal watercraft, boats, outdoor power equipment, power assist bicycles, unmanned helicopters" and more (Yamaha Celebrates 30 Years of U.S. Manufacturing). Yamaha's Newnan, Georgia, plant has produced more than 3.5 million vehicles.

ERDRICH UMFORMTECHNIK

Founded in 1962, family-owned Erdrich Umformtechnik develops and produces innovative brake, chassis, and drive parts for clients in the auto industry. The company has more than 1,750 employees worldwide. In 2013, the German company opened a plant in Dublin, Georgia, which employs around 200 people and makes parts for BMW (Bayerische Motoren Werke), Mercedes and Volkswagen, and other car manufacturers.

MANDO

Korea's Mando Corporation finished construction on a new casting facility in Meriwether County, Georgia, in 2014 that serves Mando's Machining/Electric Power Steering Gear/Electronic Stability Control Module facility in North America. The company manufactures and assembles energy-efficient automotive parts. Mando serves United States automobile manufacturers including Hyundai, BMW, Chrysler, FIAT (Fabbrica Italiana Automobili Torino), Ford, GM, Kia, and Volkswagen and others.

E-Z-GO

Magnolia Lane, with its sixty-one large trees and 330-yard path, dates back to the 1850s, but today it lines the entrance to the Augusta National Golf Course's clubhouse. Since golf legends, Bobby Jones and Clifford Roberts designed the course in 1932 and the Masters Tournament started at Augusta in 1934, people worldwide equate Augusta with golf. It's no surprise then that two of Georgia's golf cart manufacturers got their start in Augusta.

CHAPTER 7

B.F. (Bev) and Billy Dolan developed the E-Z-GO® Golf Cart in 1954. Their website notes that "In 2009, the company's Augusta, Georgia, facility was named one of *Industry Week* magazine's top 10 manufacturing plants in North America." Today, the company builds tens of thousands of golf carts annually and is part of the larger Textron Incorporated, which also builds aircraft, landscaping equipment, automotive parts, all-terrain vehicles, specialty carts used in manufacturing plants, and specialty trucks used at airports and similar sites. Brand names include Cessna, Beechcraft, Hawker, Bell Helicopter, Kautex, Arctic Cat, Jacobsen, Cushman and Textron GSE. Textron is a Fortune 500 company operating in twenty-five countries.

CLUB CAR

Club Car began in 1958 in Houston, Texas, and moved to Augusta, Georgia, in 1962. It is, since 1995, a business unit of Ingersoll Rand. It produces both gasoline-powered and electric golf carts, and also offers street legal golf carts with seat belts, turn signals, and windshields. Club Car built the first connected golf carts that may be tracked by the golf course clubhouse and that track the scores of golfers.

GREAT DANE

Great Dane got its start in 1900 by making sheet metal systems to move sawdust and wood chips in millwork plants. First known as Savannah Blow Pipe Company, in 1931, they began to manufacture trailers to carry over-the-road freight. By the 1940s, they added refrigeration to the trailers. World War II changed the company focus and added expertise and knowledge for their future operations: "The company produced about 12,000 trailers on government contracts during WWII and was awarded the Army-Navy 'E' for excellence five times." (*Great Dane*)

They changed their name to Great Dane Trailers, Incorporated, in 1958. As trucking and shipping changed, so did Great Dane: "In the early 1960s, Great Dane entered the piggyback and container market and established sales outlets in 24 states across the eastern half of the country." (*Great Dane*)

Its new Savannah office features a state-of-the-art research and development center.

Manufacturing Success in Georgia

CHAPTER 8

EARLY TIMBER HARVESTING AND WOOD PRODUCTS:

The Dodge Company, Lumber Mills, Pinola, Inc., Charles Herty, Henry Tift, Jim L. Gillis, Jr., International Paper, Graphic Packaging, Pratt, Georgia Pacific, and WestRock

EARLY HARVESTING

Trees provided early settlers with materials for shelter, fuel, shade, and food for the wildlife that lived in the forests. By Colonial times, settlers realized that they could also harvest turpentine for heating, tar for sealing ships for ocean travel, and cut lumber for housing. Virgin forests disappeared during the nineteenth century. The industry now reclaims wood from old structures and refinishes it for high-end furniture or construction work, and reforestation is the rule, not the exception.

The establishment of lumber mills along Georgia's coast enhanced a river culture that rivals Mark Twain's Great Mississippi Culture and predates it by fifty years. Georgia's Altamaha River was called "Father of Waters" by the indigenous people. The Altamaha Riverkeeper website

T. Ross Sharp wrote one of Georgia's many "Mark Twain-Like" stories about timber rafts for Tales of the Altamaha.

Harrison and the Hog Bears

Harrison Clifton was one of the grand old men of the Altamaha – born, reared, and buried in the same community where he lived each one of his eighty-nine years. He knew every fishing hole, gator pit, deer run, turkey roost, and shooting stand for thirty miles up and down the Altamaha River. He was a source of folklore, Indian stories, Civil War stories, or local stories.

Many years ago, it was the custom of every landowner living near the river to cut, saw, and float down the Altamaha a raft of timber composed of three to four hundred squared logs. It took four days and three nights to reach Darien. A little shanty would be built about the middle of the raft, where provisions, cooked food, and clothing were stored. With a little luck, fish could be caught along the way.

On one of these trips, there came up a windstorm. The shelter was blown down, and all the clothes got wet.

It was decided to "tie-up," dry the clothes, cook supper, and then drift on down the river. As soon as everyone was disrobed, the cooking began. While everyone's attention was devoted to rebuilding the raft, two hog bears took over where the cooking was going on, tore open the sack of supplies, turned over the cooking utensils, and raised havoc with everything in sight.

The man piloting the raft called out for everyone to jump on the raft [saying], "Let's go!" In the excitement, Harrison got the frying pan and left his clothes drying on a limb. The raft was out in midstream and half a mile from the landing before it occurred to anyone that Harrison's wardrobe consisted of his shoes, derby hat, and vest. Spanish moss in sufficient quantities was pulled from trees along the banks of the river, and a temporary grass skirt was made for his use in entering Darien.

To this day, that section of the river is known as "Harrison's Neck" as a reminder of the episode of Harrison and the hog bears. (Sharpe 50-51)

says, "The 137-mile Altamaha River is one of the great natural treasures of the eastern United States. Pronounced Al'ta' mahaw', the river starts at the confluence of the Ocmulgee and the Oconee Rivers near Hazlehurst and flows undammed to the Atlantic Ocean in Darien. Crossed by roads only five times, the largely undisturbed river is believed to be more than 20 million years old and pumps an average of 100,000 gallons of fresh water into the sea every second. The Altamaha's watershed is approximately 14,000 square miles, qualifying it as one of the largest river basins in the United States." There is even the famous *Altamaha-ha*, or Altie, the river monster. Like Scotland's Loch Ness monster, Altie's story lacks accepted documentation and visual evidence. Older stories include those of timber rafts. Early foresters cut and squared giant trees and lashed them together to make

Then and Now

When frontiersmen dug The Travelers Well along the Ocmulgee River in the early 1800s, they curbed (or framed) it using a large cypress tree stump. An example of this framing method can be seen at the Historic Village of Brewton-Parker College in Mount Vernon, Georgia. The Pulaski County Travelers Well, pictured in this sequence, was used over 100 years. When the wood began to decay, next-generation owners supported the structure by adding cement around the stump. In 2021, the well has water, but the tree is long gone."

rafts. Rivermen piloted the rafts from central Georgia's inland waterways like the Ocmulgee and Oconee Rivers, down the larger rivers, like the Altamaha, to Georgia's seaports. There, workers disassembled the rafts and loaded the logs on ships to be transported to customers worldwide.

Like the characters described in "Harrison and the Hog Bears", men delivered squared lumber to seaports and often walked back to the Midstate to pilot the next timber raft. The primary route from Darien inland follows the rivers. The Wilcox Traveler's Well, on the Ocmulgee River extension of this footpath, was curbed (or framed) using one of the stumps from a cut cypress. The rest of the tree would have been floated down the river and sold as lumber. As the cypress stump decayed, the owners created a

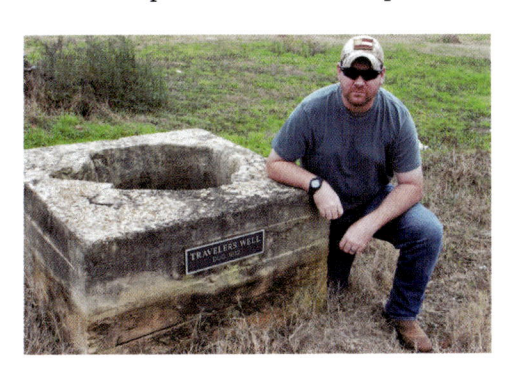

Left: A well is a hole in the ground dug to access water. A well curb is a frame or foundation built around the mouth of the hole for the safety of those who use the well. Two of the pictures show a tree stump well curb featured in a display at Brewton Parker College's Historic Village in Mount Vernon-Ailey, Georgia. Other pictures show the Traveler's Well on Old River Road in Pulaski County, Georgia. Once tree curbed, this early nineteenth well's more modern cement curb still shows the tree's imprint.

CHAPTER 8

Right: The Dodge Company built Lovely Lane Chapel on St. Simons Island for its workers at Gascoigne Bluff. Epworth by the Sea, a Methodist Retreat Center, has owned the chapel since 1950. Dodge Chapel, near Eastman and also provided by The Dodge Company, served the workers at Normandale.

Right: A William E. Dodge Statue by artist John Quincy Adams Ward stands in New York City's Bryant Park.

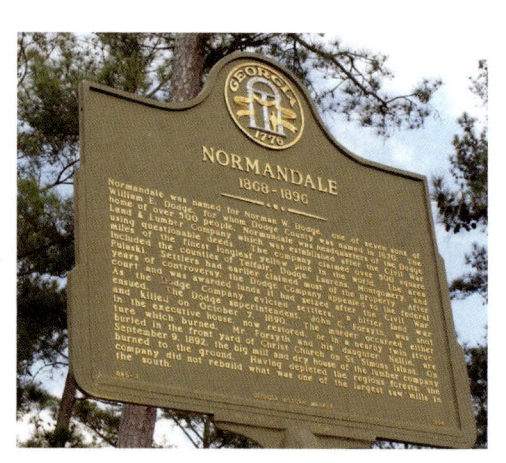

Right: The remaining Dodge Company supervisor's home near Chauncey, Georgia, in Dodge County and the Georgia State Historical Marker for Normandale on the Golden Isle Parkway, Highway 341. The murder of lumber mill superintendent John C. Forsyth occurred in a twin structure which once stood on the same property.

cement cube around the stump to support it. The cement frame, with the imprint of the tree from long ago, still stands. The two-hundred-year-old well has water in it today, and sits beside the two-lane blacktop covering the sandy trek of the timber and raftsmen. Georgia's stories of river men predate the Mississippi's simply because Georgia is one of the original colonies, and the Mississippi River Valley culture developed later.

DODGE COMPANY

William E. Dodge (1805–1883), a northern timberman who shaped the Georgia industry, was a United States representative from 1866-1867. By 1908, he founded the Phelps, Dodge Company, one of the nation's largest mining companies. Dodge invested in railroads and in what became questionable land purchases and leases involving over 300,000 acres of southeast Georgia. In 1870, Georgia established a county in the same area and named it for Dodge.

The Macon and Brunswick Railroad roughly followed the path of the Ocmulgee and Altamaha Rivers from Georgia's Queen Inland City of Macon, to the famous Marshes of Glynn, which include lands from Brunswick to Darien.

Dodge built and donated a courthouse in Dodge County, several small churches and chapels, schools, and structures to support workers, which followed nineteenth-century paternalistic mill practices. The community of Normandale was named for his brother and was home to one of the Dodge Company's inland timber

Manufacturing Success in Georgia

operations. One of the supervisor's homes still stands. Its twin structure, used for other mill staff, was a famous murder site during the timber wars. An excerpt taken from the Georgia Historical Marker reads, "The home of over 500 people, Normandale was headquarters of the Dodge Land & Lumber Company which was established after the Civil War using questionable deeds. The company claimed over 300 square miles of the finest longleaf yellow pine in the world. Settlers had earlier claimed most of the property. After years of controversy, the Dodge Company appealed to the federal court and was awarded lands it had seized after the Civil War. As the Dodge Company evicted settlers, a bitter land war ensued. The Dodge superintendent, John C. Forsyth, was shot and killed on October 7, 1890. The murder occurred either in the executive house, now restored, or in a nearby twin structure which burned. Mr. Forsyth and his daughter, Nellie, are buried in the front yard of Christ Church on St. Simons Island. On September 9, 1892, the big mill and dry house of the lumber company burned to the ground. Having depleted the region's forests, the company did not rebuild what was one of the largest sawmills in the south."

LUMBER MILLS

Lumber mills, then, appeared on the Georgia coast after the War Between the States and during Reconstruction (1870-1900). By 1880, timberland in Georgia was valued at four million dollars. River transport and railroads made exploitation of inland forests possible. Timbermen soon realized the need to replant and then schedule harvesting.

The Georgia Forestry Association claims that "Georgia is the number one forestry state in the nation, providing a myriad of economic, environmental and social benefits." *AllOnGeorgia's* website reported on December 18, 2019 that "According to a Georgia Forestry Commission report provided by the Georgia Institute of Technology's Enterprise Innovation Institute, total economic activity generated by the state's forest industry rose to $36.2

Above: A Georgia long leaf Yellow Pine and a vintage home sawmill still operated in Toombs County, Georgia

Then and Now:

Providence Canyon in Stewart County, Georgia, shows loss of land due to poor forestry and farming practices common in the nineteenth century: "The canyon consists of huge gullies sculpted of soil, not by the action of a river or stream but by rainwater runoff from farm fields." (Sanders)

New Georgia Encyclopedia writer Sigrid Sanders goes on: "Providence Canyon continues to erode and change due to surface water runoff and the undercutting force of groundwater. The clay content of sediments in the floor of the canyon makes it more resistant, and the growth of pine trees, laurel bushes, and other vegetation help to stabilize the soil, reducing the rate of vertical erosion." Providence Canyon State Park and surrounding areas include sixteen canyons, some of which are one hundred fifty feet deep. Ever-changing, The Little Grand Canyon, is listed as one of Georgia's seven natural wonders. In 2020, foresters and farmers use conservation methods to prevent erosion.

Right: Georgia's Providence Canyon was formed by erosion due to older farming methods. Realization of the causes leading to the canyon prompted soil conservation methods and crop rotation practices in the United States. Providence Canyon State Park, near Lumpkin, Georgia, invites visitors to hike into the canyon to see the layers of earth it reveals

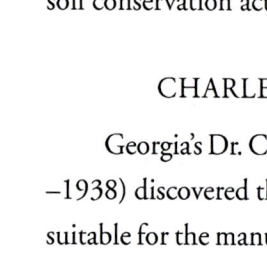

Right: A Georgia State Historic Marker on the Georgia Southern Campus, in Statesboro, honoring Charles Herty.

billion between 2017 and 2018. Additional gains were recorded in employment and wages and salaries, as documented in the '2018 Economic Benefits of Forestry in Georgia' report." It also says that "Highlights of the report show Georgia's forest industry: generated $977 million in state government revenues, and provided $110 million for the state budget (an increase of 12% over 2017)."

Harvested timberlands became farmland, and the sheer size of the state made it easy for timbermen and farmers to move to untapped lands if they depleted what was available. Land and timber conservation acts followed. President Franklin Delano Roosevelt signed the first soil conservation act in 1935.

CHARLES HERTY

Georgia's Dr. Charles H. Herty (1867–1938) discovered that southern pine was suitable for the manufacture of newsprint. Once production began, editors no longer needed to import newsprint but could buy it from Georgia manufacturers. Furthermore, the discovery proved Georgia's forests could supply enough newsprint for the entire country. Collecting other pine products like turpentine and resin was also profitable, and by 1927, Herty's cup-and-gutter system for collecting pine sap was used in Georgia and beyond. Second-growth longleaf and slash pine in Georgia and Florida, again the center of industry, supplied seventy-eight percent of America's naval stores production. Continued research included the study of pine fiber and production of high-quality products at

Manufacturing Success in Georgia

low cost. The New Georgia Encyclopedia article about Herty says that he "began working hard to secure funding for an experimental pulp and paper laboratory wherein he could test his theories regarding the substitution of cheap, fast-growing southern pine for expensive, slow-growing northern spruce in the manufacture of newspaper. By the late summer of 1931, he managed to secure an appropriation from the Georgia legislature, a matching grant from the Chemical Foundation, and a facility and free power from the city of Savannah to house what was usually dubbed the Savannah Pulp and Paper Laboratory, the first step in building a 'New South'." (Reed)

HENRY TIFT

Henry Tift (1841-1922) founded Tifton, Georgia, and "contributed for a half-century to the industrial, agricultural, financial, religious, and educational growth of his city and the well-being of its citizens." (Fair)

Tift "purchased a large tract of pine forest in Berrien County and the newly

Above: The photos show two types of Herty Cups for collecting pine tree sap and the Turpentine Industry display at the Altamaha Heritage Center in Lyons, Georgia.

Above: Henry Tift from a portrait in his home at the Georgia Museum of Agriculture and Historic Village

Left: Tifton Lumber Mill

CHAPTER 8

Above: The virgin timber of Georgia (timber that had not been cut) provided large trees for investors to sell. This trough is carved from one tree, although sections were replaced, and is on display at the Georgia Museum of Agriculture on the campus of Abraham Baldwin Agricultural College. The Henry Tift house is also part of the museum's permanent exhibit.

completed Brunswick and Western Railway. On the highest ground south of the fall line at Macon, Tift established a sawmill and a village for his workers. Eventually, he expanded into turpentine and barrel-making operations and turned his barren timberlands into farms for cotton, corn, livestock, fruit, tobacco, pecans, and sweet potatoes. When the Georgia Southern and Florida Railway intersected the Brunswick and Western at Tift's mill in 1888, the settlement was connected to Atlanta and became a boomtown." (Fair)

Tift founded the Tifton Cotton Mill, the Bank of Tifton, and Cycloneta, a model farm which developed into the Abraham Baldwin Agricultural College and the Coastal Plain Experiment Station in Tifton.

JIM L. GILLIS

Jim L. Gillis, Jr. (1916 –2018), grandson of Neil Gillis, who founded Treutlen County, Georgia, served on the Georgia Forestry Commission Board from 1977-2017. He founded the Ohoopee River Soil and Water Conservation District and served on the board for seventy-five years. The son of Jim L. Gillis, Sr., a Georgia State Senator, Jim L. Gillis, Jr., and his brother Hugh both served as Georgia State Senators. A former president of the American Turpentine Farmers Association, Jim Gillis, told Bill Consoletti, Historian for the Southeastern Society of American Foresters that "the first naval stores came out of Jamestown, Virginia, where the settlers moved in. Naval stores were one of the first exports that ever left this country. The people in North Carolina learned that if you scar a pine tree, the tree would run this resin profusely, and so they followed that. It's why North Carolina is called the 'Tar Hill State.' So before the Civil War, naval stores came primarily from North Carolina. Migration came into Wilmington, North Carolina, so that was a chief port.

"But the methods early foresters used were destructive. They harvested the rosin and gum and came back later to gather the lumber, and then they moved on. So they moved into Georgia around

Manufacturing Success in Georgia

1870. At the port in Savannah, these foresters finally developed a market for their turpentine, and the business grew from that. After Georgia, naval stores production moved into Florida, and Florida was one of the largest naval stores producers in the country. Next, it went on to Alabama, Mississippi, and East Texas. Workers would harvest naval stores from the big trees (or virgin pine), cut the timber, and leave open land.

"After the Civil War, all a southerner could sell was turpentine, rosin, and cotton, and it stayed that way up until World War II. In the 1920s, reforestation started. I know that a lot of the farmers here would take the naval stores money and try to finance their farm operation. After World War II, manufacturing came in, and people left the farm and didn't come back. They would make a dollar a day and be glad to get it. I don't think the south recovered from the Civil War until after World War II.

"After the Civil War, you had all these people, primarily blacks, and they were hungry. They were walking the roads. They were looking for jobs. So, to get turpentine workers, you would have to provide them a house, such that it was, and train them. Some were good at chipping, others for tapping the trees. Whatever the man was good at, you taught him to do that for turpentine production. Each person had different talents, so you'd develop the skill.

"There was little mechanization. You had mules and horses you to use but it was all hand labor. Naval stores production gave people employment and a place to live. It was hard work, but it was a skilled operation. At one time, we had well over a hundred families working in turpentine camps. It filled a void and really meant a lot to the people of rural Georgia." (Jim L. Gillis, Jr. Interview 23 March 2017)

Gillis and his family followed the example of James Fowler, who began planting pine trees when boll weevils destroyed his cotton crops during the 1920s. Fowler "planted more than 7 million pine seedlings on 10,000 acres in Treutlen County" and "garnered national attention from those who were interested in reforestation. Savannah scientist, Charles Herty, worked with Fowler to create

Above: Georgia's Interstate 16, also called the Jim L. Gillis Highway, passes through Soperton. Members of the Gillis family held several political offices and promoted tree farms, so Soperton holds the Million Pines Arts & Crafts Festival annually to honor that legacy.

CHAPTER 8

newsprint from his pine trees, leading to the widespread use of paper made from pine pulp. In 1933, the *Soperton News* became the first paper in the United States to print the news on pine-pulp paper." (Cooksey, Treutlen County)

Today, Georgia's Interstate 16 honors Gillis, and Soperton's Million Pines Festival celebrates Gillis and Fowler.

PINOVA, INC.

In 1911, Homer Yaryan patented a process to extract pine rosin from stumps and initiated a modern era for naval stores. Hercules bought Yaryan Naval Stores in 1920. In 1938, their "Vinsol® resin production began. Vinsol becomes the industry standard for the concrete air entrainment and asphalt emulsion markets" (Pinova). Other natural and synthetic are used in adhesives and as food additives in the early twenty-first century. The Hercules Company became Pinova in 2010 when TorQuest Partners acquired it. A French Company, DRT (Dérivés Résiniques et Terpéniques), purchased Pinova in 2016.

THE LANGDALE COMPANY

The Langdale Company, in Valdosta, began "with one crop of turpentine timber on the western edge of the Okefenokee Swamp in 1894, and has grown into a highly diversified enterprise that includes forestry, forest products and other affiliate companies that span the automotive, banking, hospitality and land development industries." (The Langdale Company)

In 2009, the company planted its one hundred millionth seedling. Founder John Wesley Langdale began with turpentine. Following his death, his sons incorporated as the J.W. Langdale Company in 1919. By 1937, Harley Langdale, Sr., has crews "working nearly three million trees for turpentine and operating twenty-five turpentine camps and stills," and Harvey Langdale, Jr. graduated from Forestry School at the University of Georgia. He was the first person in Lowndes County to study forestry as a science." (History: 1894 – The Seed is Planted)

INTERNATIONAL PAPER

International Paper, headquartered in Memphis, Tennessee, "employs more than 50,000 people worldwide and serves more than 25,000 customers in 150 countries" and "is one of the world's leading producers of fiber-based packaging, pulp, and paper." (*International Paper*)

In Georgia, International Paper produces corrugated boxes and packaging in

Manufacturing Success in Georgia

Columbus, Forest Park, Griffin, Lithonia, and Savannah. International Paper also makes gaylord boxes, bulk bins, corrugated sheets, retail displays, and "packaging products that protect and promote goods, enable worldwide commerce and keep consumers safe; pulp for diapers, tissue, and other personal hygiene products that promote health and wellness; and papers that facilitate education and communication." (*International Paper*)

GRAPHIC PACKAGING

Graphic Packaging currently owns and operates Macon's only paper mill. Once a producer of containerboard only, the company manufactures "paper-based packaging for some of the world's most recognized brands of food, beverage, foodservice, household, personal care, and pet care products" in seventy facilities worldwide: "Graphic Packaging International's history extends more than 100 years, as numerous legacy companies have joined forces to create an ever-evolving corporation." (Graphic Packaging)

One of those legacy companies was Georgia Kraft. In 1974, Dianne Dent-Wilcox, co-author for *Manufacturing Success in Georgia*, wrote her first report on the papermaking process for a tenth-grade assignment. It provided an imaginary tour of how Georgia's pine trees become paper.

GEORGIA KRAFT COMPANY: PINE TREES, PULP AND PAPER - MARCH 30, 1974

We are standing in one of the forests of Georgia Kraft Company. It is ready for harvesting, and the machinery is coming

---

Then and Now

Once, timber barons instructed their workers to clear cut the trees on a property and move to the next property. The newer practice of cutting trees and planting new ones before moving to other forests helped replenish wildlife habitats, controlled erosion. It provided lumber companies with more available timber and pulpwood in the coming years. Because wood can be used even if it is reduced to fiber, recycling was natural in the industry. Sawdust can be pressed into pellets, and used in specialty furnaces to heat homes.

Wood chips can be used to make particle board or paper. Paper recycling mixes old paper with water and chemicals to break it down into pulp, which can be processed into new paper. 'Paper Recycling Facts' posted by the University of Southern Indiana, states that "Each ton (2000 pounds) of recycled paper can save 17 trees, 380 gallons of oil, three cubic yards of landfill space, 4000 kilowatts of energy, and 7000 gallons of water. This represents a 64% energy savings, a 58% water savings, and 60 pounds less of air pollution." The University of Valdosta's proposed recycling policy confirms this data. The University of Southern Indiana adds that "Paper recycling reuses a renewable resource that sequesters carbon and helps reduce greenhouse gas emissions. Greenhouse gas reductions result from avoided methane emissions. In addition, recovering paper extends the fiber supply."

to start the operation. The machine that cuts the trees is a hydro-pneumatic jack.

This machine pinches the tree in two. The tree falls onto another machine that loads the trees into a truck to be taken to the mill. Georgia Kraft also buys logs and chips from other companies. "Georgia Kraft uses four major native varieties of pine: longleaf, shortleaf, slash, and loblolly for their paper." (How Container Board is Made)

Georgia Kraft has full-time foresters working to replant trees after the cutting is finished. They also use block, selective, and other cutting methods that preserve the land. We will follow the truck to Georgia Kraft.

On arrival, the truck is weighed. It will be weighed again when it leaves. It goes to the woodpile, where it is unloaded by one of the giant cranes. The wood is raked onto a conveyor and goes to the saws to be cut into lengths. Any log that is fourteen inches in diameter or wider is cut into fourteen feet lengths, and sold to Georgia Pacific to be used as plywood.

The rest of the trees is debarked and chipped by the 24-inch chipper. The chips are ready for storage. Other logs are cut into lengths of fifty-six inches and taken to the barking drum. The barking drum is fifteen feet in diameter and fifty feet long. The logs are tumbled until all of the bark has been removed. The logs are washed and then taken to the chipper. Five seconds later, they are chips and taken to the chip storage tanks. After storage, the chips are taken to the blow pit. This action breaks the chips into individual fibers. The

Manufacturing Success in Georgia

fibers are then taken to the digesters. In the digesters, the fibers are cooked in chemicals and are turned into pulp. The pulp then continues through four stages of washers and then stored until needed:

'When needed, the pulp is pumped through refiners which prepare the surface of the fibers to make them bond together properly on the paper machine." (How Container Board is Made)

From the refiners, the pulp is taken to the headbox. By this time, the pulp has been changed to stock, which is three hundred parts water to one part fiber. "The stock is pumped to a headbox from which it flows evenly onto the fast-moving screen of the Fourdrinier wire." (How Container Board is Made)

Until recently, the Fourdrinier wire was made of copper wire, which had to be changed every one to two weeks. This wire costs $4,500. Now a plastic Fourdrinier wire is used, which costs $11,000 but only has to be changed once in sixty days. It drains the water from the stock: "The sheet is picked up from the wire on endless belts of heavy woolen felt which carry the wet sheet through heavy press rollers that squeeze out more water." (How Container Board is Made)

Afterward, the press section sheet of paper is moved into the after dryers. There are four sections of these dyers with one hundred two dryers in all. Each dryer is a drum five feet by twenty feet, and uses tremendous steam pressure to dry the paper. Having passed through the dryers, the board is then "ironed smooth between heavy calendar rolls and is wound into a roll at the reel." (How Container Board is Made)

About ten tons of paper is wound on the reel every twenty minutes, then taken to the winder by a twenty-five-ton crane. The winder rewinds the paper into "small lengths to meet the customer's requirements." (How Container Board is Made)

The rolls are then marked, weighed, and shipped to the customer either by train or truck.

In the next few years, the size of the Georgia Kraft Company is expected to double. Georgia Kraft not only makes paper, but also sells lumber for plywood. It also sells enough turpentine and tall oil (used in highway construction) to make the payroll. Also, until recently, the plant generated all of its electricity.

The plant also refines and reuses its chemicals and water.

The plant has also installed millions of dollars of smoke filters to help control air pollution: The company has led the way in providing adequate protection for the rivers and streams from which it draws the necessary water for operation. As for land conservation, Georgia Kraft has full-time foresters working to keep the woodlands plentiful.

Every safety measure is taken at the mill, too. A registered nurse is on duty twenty-four hours a day, hardhats must be worn in the woodyard, and warning signs are posted at all dangerous locations.

Safety lines must be worn on certain jobs. Last year, the company received the

President's Safety Award, and has received many others.

The paper mill is growing. The building was constructed in 1948 to produce about six hundred tons of paper daily. This period has averaged nine hundred thirty-six tons daily. The number of employees at Georgia Kraft is about six hundred. Women now work in the maintenance department, which includes the pipe shop, carpenter shop, machine shop, millwright shop, electric shop, automotive shop, paint shop, fabrication shop, and the service crew, which maintains the railroad. The buildings cover an area of about seven acres. The wood yard covers an area of about twenty-five acres.

Georgia Kraft has three divisions, the Mead at Macon, the Krannert at Rome, and Mahrt at Mahrt, Alabama. The division manager at Mead is Mr. Bill Davey, the division manager at Krannert is Mr. Ed Wilson, and the division manager at Mahrt is Mr. Bob Bradley.

I hope that you learned as much as I did on our imaginary tour.

BIBLIOGRAPHY

Charles E. Dent (1932-2017), Interview and Tour. February 22, 1974.

"How Containerboard is Made." Georgia Kraft Company Pamphlet.

PRATT

Recycling prevents the waste of useful materials by converting them into new materials or objects. It saves energy, reduces greenhouse gases, limits water and air pollution, and saves space used for landfills. Georgia-based Pratt Industries recycles paper, plastic, and metal collected from residences, communities, schools, and commercial and industrial plants. They send used newspapers, magazines, catalogs, office paper, books, corrugated cardboard, and mail to four paper mills who produces a hundred percent recycled packaging paper in Conyers, Georgia; New York, New York; Valparaiso, Indiana; and Shreveport, Louisiana.

Pratt also recycles low-density polyethylene film (LDPE film), polyethylene terephthalate (PET) and steel banding, pallets, plastic containers, aluminum cans, and steel cans. The company grew from one plant in the 1980s to maintaining "manufacturing plants in more than 25 states" (About Pratt). Pratt, the 5th largest corrugated paper packaging plant in the United States, diverts "Over 3 million tons of materials from landfill every year. It has 19 modern Material Recovery Facilities or other recycling plants, and an operational footprint from New York to California." (About Pratt)

The company "has been honored by environmental leaders such as former Vice President Al Gore, former British Prime Minister Tony Blair, Ted Turner, the Climate Group and Global Green for spreading the word that recycling is an important weapon against climate change." (About Pratt)

GEORGIA PACIFIC

Georgia Pacific is another well known "multinational corporation that manufactures paper, pulp, packaging,

Left: Georgia Pacific Lumber

tissue, building products, and construction-related chemicals." (Griffin)

It employs 7,320 people, and Georgia Pacific calculates that this means an additional 21,920 indirectly created jobs. (About Us, *Georgia Pacific*).

Georgia Pacific's facilities include the Norcross Innovation Institute, Rome Lumber, Atlanta GP Center, Augusta Corrugated, Warrenton Lumber, Albany Corrugated, Albany Lumber, Rincon-Savannah River, Savannah Gypsum, Brunswick Cellulose plants, Decatur Gypsum, and Decatur Chemical Labs.

The company produces building materials made of wood and gypsum, adhesives, resins, pulp, and consumer products that include "napkins, paper towels, bath tissue, facial tissue, and disposable foodservice products," while maintaining sustainable forests and using environmentally responsible practices. It is currently a subsidiary of Koch.

WESTROCK

America's second-largest packaging company, WestRock, is headquartered in Atlanta and has fifteen billion dollars in annual revenue, with forty-two thousand employees in thirty countries. The company maintains operations in Asia, Australia, Europe, North America, and South America. WestRock paper products include containerboard, corrugated containers, displays, folding cartons, Kraft paper, paperboard, partitions and protective packaging, pulp, and actively trains its employees in new recycling technologies.

CHAPTER 8

Right: This model of Epps' 1912 Monoplane is in the Robins Air Force Base Museum of Aviation.

CHAPTER 9

AVIATION

Hartsfield-Jackson Atlanta International Airport, Charles Lindberg, Ben Epps, Maule Air, Thrush Aircraft, Lockheed Martin, Gulfstream, Delta, Eastern, The Museum of Aviation, The Entomopter, and Spaceport Camden

HARTSFIELD-JACKSON ATLANTA INTERNATIONAL AIRPORT

You can hear Georgians say: "Whether you are going to heaven or hell, you must go through Hartfield-Jackson Airport in Atlanta, first." Founded in 1925, Hartsfield-Jackson covers 4,700 acres and is the second busiest airport in the world. The airport handled 107 million passengers in 2018 which is around 275,000 per day. Centrally located, about eighty percent of the United States population is within a two-hour flight from Atlanta.

Hartsfield-Jackson's parallel runways, which are 9,000 to 12,390 feet long, allow between ninety and hundred flights to land or depart each hour. Two have "Category III Instrument Landing Systems (ILS) that provide precise radio beams for aircraft to follow down to the runway so that the most modern aircraft can land themselves during weather conditions in which the visibility and ceiling prevent the pilots from seeing the runway until they have landed." (Pritchett)

Atlanta's Air Traffic Control uses a system based on the distance an aircraft is from the field. Those on the runway and just after takeoff work with the Atlanta Air Traffic Control Tower (ATCT). The Terminal Radar Control facility (TRACON) in Peachtree City helps pilots navigate through northeast, northwest, southwest, and southeast corner posts about forty miles away from the airport. Aircrafts operating at travel altitudes work with the Air Route Traffic Control Center (Atlanta ARTCC) in Hampton, which controls air traffic "over most of Georgia and Alabama, extending north through North Carolina and Tennessee into Kentucky, West Virginia, and Virginia." (Pritchett)

CHARLES LINDBERG

Charles Augustus Lindbergh (1902–1974), the United States Air Mail Pilot, leaped from obscurity to worldwide fame in 1927 by making a nonstop flight from New York to Paris. However, Lindbergh flew his first solo flight from a former World War I training site located in Americus, to Montgomery, Alabama, in 1923. The Georgia State Historic Marker at Souther Field says "The Lone Eagle first flew solo in early May 1923 from Souther Field."

Lindbergh had come to Americus "to purchase a surplus aircraft from the World War I training center. He chose a Curtiss JN4 'Jenny'. He got the plane with a brand-new OX-5 engine, a fresh coat of olive drab dope, and an extra twenty-gallon fuel tank for $500. Lindbergh had less than twenty hours of instruction when he soloed. He practiced take-offs and landings for a week; then having filled up with forty gallons of gas, he set course for Montgomery, Alabama, to start his barnstorming career. Four years later, Lindbergh flew alone in the 'Spirit of St. Louis' from New York to Paris, and into aviation history." There is a seven-foot bronze statue of Lindberg, made at the University of Georgia, standing at Souther Field today. In 1927, and "largely through the efforts of Atlanta city alderman William B. Hartsfield (a pilot and aviation enthusiast), Lindbergh returned to Georgia on October 11. Flying from Jacksonville, Florida, via McRae, Vidalia, and Millen, the Spirit of St. Louis landed at Candler Field in Hapeville at two o'clock on a drizzly afternoon." (Zainaldin, Lindberg)

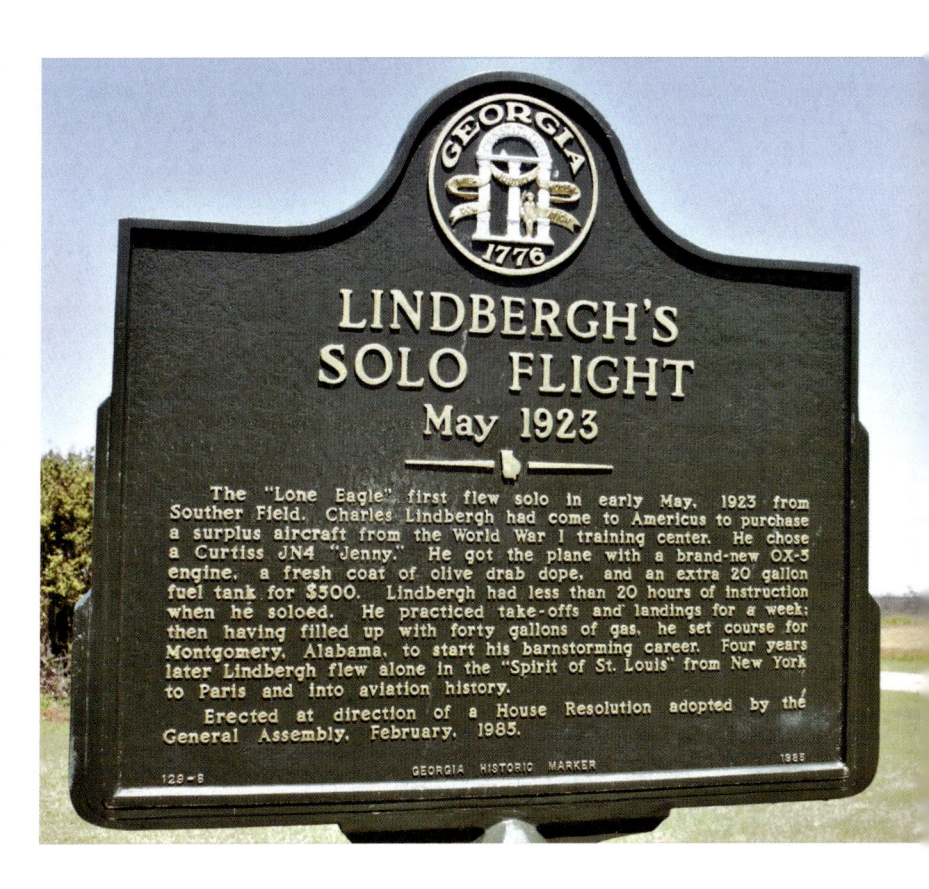

Above: Lindbergh Historical Marker

Right: Ben T. Epps (February 20, 1888, Oconee County, Georgia - October 16, 1937), known as "Georgia's First Aviator" was an American aviation pioneer.

GEORGIA'S AVIATION PIONEER, BEN EPPS

Ben Epps (1888-1937) was the first Georgian to build and fly an airplane. This Oconee County born mechanic, "Inspired by the success of the Wright brothers in 1903, ... In 1907 the nineteen-year-old Epps flew his first plane at an open field in Athens." (Hudson)

Epps changed the Wright brothers' design, and his "first flight was about 100 yards long, with an altitude of 50 feet. A replica of one of his later inventions, the Epps 1912 Monoplane, is on display at the Museum of Aviation in Warner Robins." (Hudson)

Epps was exempt from service in World War I because he had a large family. He and L. Monte Rolfe, an aviator, established the Rolfe-Epps Flying Service using army surplus planes. They taught generations of Georgia pilots, and established Georgia's Epps Flying Field which is now the site of Athens-Ben Epps Airport. The family continued Epps aviation legacy: "His eldest son, Ben Epps Jr. (1916-2001), at age thirteen, was at the time the youngest pilot ever to solo and attracted so much attention that President Herbert Hoover invited him to the White House. The Epps father-and-son team became popular "barnstorming" stars of stunt flying and air races in Georgia. Epps died in an airplane crash on a test flight near Athens in 1937. His son Ben Jr. joined the U.S. Army Air Corps, and in World War II (1941-45) he flew a C-46 over the Himalayan Mountains, providing supplies to the "Flying Tigers" in China, Burma, and India. In 1994, Ben Epps Jr. was enshrined in the Georgia Aviation Hall of Fame, in which his father had been honored as a charter member." (Hudson)

The family still owns Epps Aviation, based at DeKalb Peachtree Airport in Atlanta.

MAULE AIR

Maule Air, in Moultrie, produces single-engine, four-place Short Takeoff or Landing (STOL) aircraft: "The STOL abilities of the Maule series have proven useful in terrain ranging from Canadian lakes to the Alaskan bush to the dense jungles of Brazil." (Bellury, "Maule") Today, founders B.D. and June Maule are both members of the Georgia Aviation Hall of Fame, B.D. Maule in 1992, and June Maule in 1999. The Georgia Aviation Hall of Fame is located at the Museum of Aviation in Warner Robins, Georgia.

Manufacturing Success in Georgia

B. D. "Maule was a dedicated engineer and designer. Among his innovations were specialty television antennas, towers, and rotator parts, and a nondestructive fabric tester approved and still utilized by the Federal Aviation Administration (FAA)." (Bellury)

B.D. Maule began working with aircraft in 1929 and continued until he died in 1995. June, then, served as company president until 2005 when she was eighty-eight years of age. Their children and grandchildren still work for Maule Air.

The family chose Spence Field in Moultrie, Georgia for their base of operations in 1968. Today, "Maule Air produces twenty standard models of the STOL aircraft, eighteen with piston engines and two with turbine engines. In 2003 Maule Air introduced the M-9-230 at the Experimental Aircraft Association Oshkosh AirVenture and became the first U.S. aircraft, original equipment manufacturer, to utilize the SMA SR305 Jet-A powered diesel engine. The M-9-230 serves as either a five-seat passenger plane or a two-seat cargo hauler. Because of their unique flight characteristics, Maule planes were chosen for use in three motion pictures: *Cannonball Run* (1981), *Gone Fishin'* (1997), and *Speed 2* (1997)." (Bellury)

THRUSH AIRCRAFT

Thrush Aircraft help with "sowing rice, feeding shrimp, top dressing timber, spraying crop canopies, drug eradication, border surveillance, transporting fuel to remote locations, combating oil spills, and mosquito and locust control. Founded in 1966 when North American Rockwell Corporation purchased the product line of Snow Aeronautical, this agricultural aircraft manufacturer moved to Albany, Georgia, in 1970. Then, "in the 1970s, Rockwell sold production rights for their agricultural aircraft to Ayres Corporation and success continued for several years. Twenty-six years later, a forward-thinking businessman from Atlanta purchased the assets of the then defunct Ayres Corporation and renamed the company Thrush Aircraft." (Thrush Aircraft)

Thrush Aircraft operates "under the FAA-approved Production Certificate 5S0 and meets Mil-I-45208 inspection system requirements, Mil-Q-9858A quality system requirements and Mil-Standard-45662 calibration system requirements: "Over the years, a number of aircraft ground-breaking projects have been produced under contract at our Albany facility, including the Myers 200, Lark Darter, CalAir A9, and A9B, Rockwell 112, and all Thrush aircraft since 1970." (Thrush)

Thrush recently developed a firefighting plane that is now in use by Georgia Forestry. This saves taxpayers' money because of its efficiency and eliminating the use of firefighting bulldozers. Mark McDonald became the new CEO of Thrush in 2019.

LOCKHEED MARTIN

The Lockheed Martin Aeronautical Systems Company in Marietta continues the aeronautical tradition of Georgia, which began during World War II. Bell, Lockheed's predecessor in Georgia,

Right: Lockheed C-130 Hercules

produced B-29 bombers for World War II. Lockheed initially refurbished B-29s for the Korean Conflict, worked with Boeing and Douglas to build B-17 Flying Fortresses, and manufactured Boeing-designed B-47s. Other famous Lockheed Martin designs include the C-130 Hercules, C-141 Starlifter and C-5 Galaxy. "In 1993 Lockheed purchased General Dynamics' tactical military aircraft operation, with headquarters in Fort Worth, Texas, where the F-16 fighter plane was manufactured. General Dynamics was already teamed with Lockheed and Boeing in developing the F-22 Raptor. Shortly afterward, Lockheed chief executive officer Daniel M. Tellep initiated negotiations with Martin Marietta, another venerable company that traced its roots back to aviation pioneer Glenn Martin. By the 1990s Lockheed, America's second-largest defense contractor, and Martin Marietta, the nation's third-largest, were similar in size. Unlike Lockheed, however, Martin Marietta had abandoned aircraft manufacturing, choosing instead to focus on aerospace engineering and missile technology. In March 1995 stockholders of the two companies approved a $10 billion merger, creating the Lockheed Martin Corporation, with headquarters in Bethesda, Maryland. The Georgia operation was renamed Lockheed Martin Aeronautical Systems Company (LMASC). In 2000 Lee E. Rhyant, a Georgia native, became the general manager of LMASC. In the early twenty-first century, the facility was able to stay in business through Pentagon contracts for C-130Js and F-22 fighter planes. It also had a contract to modernize all 111 of the air force's C-5 fleet. In 2005 the workforce stood at 7,800, and on May 16, 2006, the company held a ceremony in Marietta to display the first of the C-5M Super Galaxies." (Scott)

Today, Lockheed Martin works through four major business segments: Aeronautics, Missiles and Fire Control, Rotary and Mission Systems, and Space.

GULFSTREAM

Gulfstream Aerospace Corporation, a subsidiary of General Dynamics, operates in Savannah and Brunswick, Georgia. Other locations include Wisconsin, Texas, Nevada, California, Massachusetts, Florida, England, and Mexico. Gulfstream is the largest manufacturing employer in the state with about 10,000 in Georgia and 18,000 around the world. Grumman Aircraft Engineering Company began to produce military aircraft. Later, it moved into the commercial market and produced the first aircraft with the Gulfstream brand in 1957.

The prop-driven Gulfstream I "advertised maximum speed of 350 miles per hour at 25,000 feet and a range of 2,200 miles. The cabin seated twelve comfortably and more if the need arose. The initial price, in 1958, was $845,000." (Bellury, Gulfstream)

In 2020, the company manufactured the Gulfstream G700, with a top speed of Mach 0.925, Gulfstream G280, Gulfstream G650ER, and Gulfstream G500 which range in cost from $11 million to $46 million (Gulfstream Aerospace).

Gulfstream also contributes to community and education: "The company has supported and partnered with the Georgia Institute of Technology's branch campus in Savannah, Savannah Technical College, and the Savannah College of Art and Design, and many of Gulfstream's executives have served on local boards. The company has also contributed to the arts, and the Mighty Eighth Air Force Museum in Pooler, located a few miles from the Gulfstream manufacturing plant." (Bellury)

In 2020, the company saw an increase in Maintenance, Repair, Overhaul (MRO) or repair, service, and inspection of aircraft. It is essentially the maintenance activities

Left: Gulfstream G700

that take place to ensure the safety and airworthiness of all aircraft by international standards. Mark Burns, President of Gulfstream, was a keynote speaker at the 2018 Georgia Manufacturing Alliance Summit.

DELTA

Another of Georgia's aviation chuckles involves outsiders who berate the South, or more precisely, Georgia. Georgians will often smile and say, "Delta is ready when you are." Taken from a 1970s advertising campaign, the comment simply means that people who come here should love our state or leave it. Delta branded itself so well that the commercial phrase moved to common culture. In 2015, Atlanta-based Delta Air Lines was "the world's largest in terms of passengers, with operations around the world." (Zainaldin, Delta)

Since 1928, the company has modernized and expanded to meet the needs of commercial travelers. It began as an effort to boost agriculture, another one of Georgia's economic successes: "Delta's origins can be traced to a historic decision by B. R. Coad and C. E. Woolman. Coad was an employee of the U.S. Department of Agriculture's field laboratory in Tallulah, Louisiana; Woolman worked for its extension service. They worked on finding a solution to the boll weevil infestation of cotton crops and concluded that the 'dusting' of an insecticide powder from the air would be the most effective form of treatment." (Zainaldin, Delta)

Delta's fleet best shows the company's history. In 1948, Delta used the propeller drive Douglas DC-6, which had four engines and cruised at 328 mph. Next were the DC-3s, DC-7s, Convair 440s, DC-8 jets, and Convair 880s, then Delta moved to all jets in 1970. Then came Boeing 727s, DC-10s, Lockheed L-1011 Tristars, Boeing 767-300ERs, MD-11s, and Boeings 767-400ERs. The company now provides global service due in part to its "'hub and spoke' system of connecting flights, which is now used by most of the major airlines." (Zainaldin, Delta)

Though Delta experienced debilitating losses in the early 2000s, strategies to reduce costs and increase efficiency saved it.

Delta Tech Ops is a division of Delta Air Lines and is a full-service aviation maintenance, repair, and overhaul (MRO) provider with more than 11,000 seasoned professionals system-wide." (Delta Tech Ops)

The company's operation in Atlanta covers 2.7 million square feet, and its operations in Minneapolis-St. Paul covers 345,600 square feet. Delta Tech Ops is a founding member of the SkyTeam Airline Alliance.

EASTERN

Eastern Air Lines began in Philadelphia, Pennsylvania, as Pitcairn Aviation in the 1920s to meet a United States Airmail contract. It became Eastern in the 1930s, offering passenger service, and developing a business hub in Atlanta, but ultimately liquidated in 1991. Notable aviators who served at Eastern include Eddie Rickenbacker, a World War I (1917-18) fighter, NASA astronaut Frank Borman, and Rusty Heard, who taught Paul Tibbets (best known as the pilot who flew the B-29 Superfortress known as the *Enola Gay* when it dropped Little Boy, the first of two atomic bombs used in warfare, on the Japanese city of Hiroshima) to fly. Rickenbacker added Douglas DC-2s, DC-3s, DC-4s, DC-6s, and DC-7s to Eastern's fleet. In 1961, Eastern initiated a shuttle service connecting Boston, Washington, D.C., and New York. It was the first air shuttle in the industry. Jet service at Eastern began in the 1960s with the Boeing 727 and continued by adding the Lockheed L-1011: "In 2016, the Southern Labor Archives at Georgia State University debuted the Eastern Air Lines Digital Collection." (Zainaldin, Eastern)

This means that photographs and written records related to Eastern Air Lines are now digitally preserved, and accessible on the internet.

THE MUSEUM OF AVIATION

The Museum of Aviation on Robins Air Force Base at Warner Robins, Georgia, is one of Georgia's treasures. This fifty-one-acre site attracts more than half a million visitors annually: "Most of the aircraft are stored in a special maintenance facility; many, especially the largest, are located in an outdoor area." (Zainaldin, Museum)

- The museum was incorporated by the Southeastern Museum of Aviation Foundation in 1981 to preserve the heritage and tradition of military and civilian aviation in the Southeastern United States.
- Foster the study of aerospace history in the Southeastern United States.
- Stimulate esprit de corps by telling the military and civilian aviation story through displays of historical significance.
- Support the Air Force recruiting program and enlistment by informing the public and youth of the Southeastern

Above: A C-141 Starlifter model with the Museum of Aviation logo, an F-16 Fighting Falcon and a P40 Kittybomber, at the Robins Air Force Base Museum of Aviation

CHAPTER 9
91

United States through educational exhibits that present the history of the Air Force.

- Foster the economic growth of Middle Georgia, the State of Georgia, and the Southeastern United States.

The museum features "more than 70 aircraft, missiles, and cockpits dating from a replica of an early 1896 glider to modern-era aircraft such as the B-1 bomber, the SR-71 Blackbird, the U-2 Dragon Lady, and the F-15 Eagle." (*Guide to the Robins Region Georgia*)

The Museum of Aviation at Robins Air Force Base also displays a "Flying Tigers P-40 Warhawk, a B-25 Mitchell bomber, and a P-51 Mustang" along with an "EC-135 once used by General Norman Schwarzkopf in Operation Desert Storm, a Vietnam War-era F-4D Phantom MiG Killer, an A-10 Thunderbolt, an F-105D Thunderchief, a C-130E cargo aircraft, and an MH-53 special operations helicopter that saw sustained combat operations in the Middle East." (*Guide to the Robins Region Georgia*)

THE ENTOMOPTER

Georgia's aviation expanded into space exploration technology, mimicking insects. The device used is called an Entomopter: "a robotic 'artificial insect' that would fly and navigate using two sets of flapping wings powered by a chemically fueled artificial muscle. Under development at the Georgia Institute of Technology, the Entomopter— its name arising from the Greek entomon, 'insect,' and pteron, 'wing'—grew out of a competition to develop palm-sized 'micro flyers' for such military applications as the exploration of caves, bunkers, and other structures. Building on five years of study and support from agencies including the Defense Advanced Research Projects Agency, the concept has since been adapted to a more unusual mission: exploring the planet Mars." (Toon)

China filed two copyrights for Entomopter technology in 2019, and the United States filed one copyright in 2019.

The Entomopter overcomes obstacles of other low flying vehicles by using insect-like wings which allow it to operate in thin atmospheric conditions, with lack of oxygen, and on rocky terrain. So far, using the Entomopter in space is conceptual, but major groups including NASA continue its development.

SPACEPORT CAMDEN

The Camden County Board of Commissioners, the Camden County Joint Development Authority, the Georgia Department of Economic Development, the Georgia Department of Transportation, and other State and Federal Agencies, as well as commercial space companies, are working to develop a Spaceport in Woodbine.

According to Cristen Conger of HowStuffWorks, "Spaceports are basically airports for space vehicles. The United States already has a handful of them, most notably the Kennedy Space Center in Florida. In Virginia, NASA partners with the Mid-Atlantic Regional Spaceport. Along with two wholly commercial spaceports in Mojave,

California, and Kodiak, Alaska, these spaceports serve as research and testing hubs that launch rockets and space shuttles. Most often, the rocket's freight, or payload, consists of satellites and scientific research equipment rather than people."

The planned spaceport will establish "common operating environments for launch operators who wish to reach" both the Spaceport Camden and the Alaska Aerospace Corporation (AAC) orbits. In December of 2019, supporters of the spaceport withdrew their license application to change the size of the vehicles they plan to launch. In 2020, they are taking other steps to prepare. On June 15, 2020, organizers announced the Memorandum of Understanding (MOU) that "will grant customers access to both high and low-inclination orbits." ("Launching America's Future Today: Georgia's Space Coast")

Left: SpacePort Camden Logo

Woodbine plans to offer training as well. On May 11, 2020, Opifex Global and Camden County signed an MOU "to explore commercial astronaut training facilities near the proposed Spaceport Camden. Opifex Global utilizes the same quality curriculum, simulators, and training devices that people have come to expect from the space program and adapted them to train commercial astronauts."

CHAPTER 9

Above: High Tech Assembly at KIA

CHAPTER 10

What the Future Holds: High-Speed Broadband for Everyone

GALILEO, Hargray-ComSouth, Viasat, Southwire, Nanotechnology, Georgia's Technology Corridors, Technology on a Georgia Air Force Base, Georgia Tech, and SoftWear

HIGH SPEED BROADBAND FOR EVERYONE

In common lore, there are two Georgias: Atlanta, and the rest of the state. Though not entirely true, the statement illustrates profound differences in the urban and rural areas of the largest state east of the Mississippi. High-speed broadband internet access, readily available in urban areas, is an adventure elsewhere. Access often determines the success of business ventures, education, prosperity, and healthcare. The 2019-2020 COVID-19 pandemic accentuated this inequality. COVID was not really on Georgia's radar in 2019. Georgia's population/businesses did not consider the impact of a COVID-19 outbreak

Manufacturing Success in Georgia

until January and February of 2020, when it started to move out of China. By May 2020, the use of remote or online meetings for business, healthcare, and education was standard practice.

Increased broadband investments in rural Georgia stem from the April 2017 establishment of the Interagency Task Force on Agriculture and Rural Prosperity whose objective it is "to identify legislative, regulatory, and policy changes that could promote agriculture and prosperity in rural communities." Access to high-speed internet supports "business development; housing; community facilities such as schools, public safety, and health care." (USDA Press)

In 2018, The Georgia Assembly passed the Achieving Connectivity Everywhere (ACE) Act (SB 402): "The legislation calls for promoting and deploying broadband services to unserved areas throughout the state, with minimum speeds of 25 Mbps for downloads and 3 Mbps for uploads. The team continues to build a strong foundation to extend broadband services across the state, strengthen rural Georgia, and make Georgia the number-one state for small businesses." (Georgia Technology Authority)

In May 2019, Mark Niesse reported in *The Atlanta Journal-Constitution* that "1.6 million Georgia residents lack fast internet connections." The state is working to correct this for the hospitals, businesses, schools, and farms that need to be online. The global COVID-19 pandemic brought greater attention to the issue when education switched from in-classroom to virtual classes online, and non-essential employees were asked to work from home. Virtual communication became the new normal. The legislation now allows Georgia's electric membership cooperatives or EMC's to sell online access. For now, Georgia's broadband plan is to "map every location in the state to determine what areas lack internet access, create a framework for future government funding of internet construction, and provide state assistance to internet providers and local governments." (Niesse)

On February 21, 2020, "Agriculture Secretary Sonny Perdue announced a $5 million investment in two, high-speed broadband infrastructure projects that will create or improve rural e-Connectivity for 1,221 rural households, 32 pre-subscribed businesses and 20 pre-subscribed farms in McIntosh and Evans counties in Georgia. This is one of many funding announcements in the first round of the United States Department of Agriculture's (USDA) ReConnect Pilot Program investments." (USDA Press)

In May 2020, Olivia Bauer posted that "people across our state continue to stay home to combat the spread of COVID-19, and many have increasingly relied on broadband internet service to maintain connections to their work, their education, and their health." Bauer, an intern for a podcast about Georgia politics called PeachPod, and a student at the University of Georgia, argues that "this crisis will illustrate that high-speed internet access is a right, not a luxury. It affects the education, healthcare, and economic stability of everyone." Office workers who can work from home, which only make up 29% of the workforce, can "keep their jobs by working from home with video teleconferencing. With the help of a directory of internet access points, students are transitioning to distance learning. And those experiencing non-Coronavirus ailments are being treated through online communication with healthcare providers. But the shift to digital life is not smooth for everyone. Most of those who lack broadband access live in rural Georgia, and access to high-speed internet has become crucial for students completing assignments at home, both before and during the COVID-19 pandemic." (Bauer)

Bauer concludes her article by saying, "high-speed internet connects people socially, and provides access to entertainment and information. It connects us to art and diversity. COVID-19 is illuminating the technological dimension of equality, and the discourse around internet access will be altered permanently."

GALILEO

Education is a key to productivity, also. At one point in time, scholars used brick and mortar libraries exclusively. As internet resources grew, Georgia developed GALILEO, a collection of more than fifty databases, and one of the earliest statewide library systems in the United States: "The primary objective of GALILEO (Georgia Library Learning Online), is to utilize available technology to electronically deliver uniform and universal access to extensive educational resources to everyone in Georgia. The intent is to make it easier for libraries to share resources and to equalize access to information throughout the state. Through the use of sophisticated technology, GALILEO connects all of Georgia's communities regardless of location or economic considerations." (Williams, Jayne)

Furthermore, "distance learners can research in a fully functioning virtual library that can be reached from any computer with Internet access." (Williams, Jayne)

GALILEO and similar online library resources allow students to conduct high-level research remotely. It enhances learning for the entire state, the two Georgias, both urban and rural.

HARGRAY-COMSOUTH

ComSouth is one of the companies providing phone and Internet services to underserved areas. It is "an integrated independent telecommunications company serving the cities of Hawkinsville, Perry, Fort Valley, Cochran, Unadilla, Pinehurst, Marshallville, Kathleen, Bonaire, and Warner Robins, as well as parts of Pulaski, Houston, Dodge, Dooly, Bleckley, Peach, and Macon Counties; provides state-of-the-art technology to deliver a variety of communication and broadband services including fiber-optic fiber to the premise, local, and long-distance telephone, and high-speed broadband internet with digital highspeed capabilities." (ComSouth)

Antenna Systems

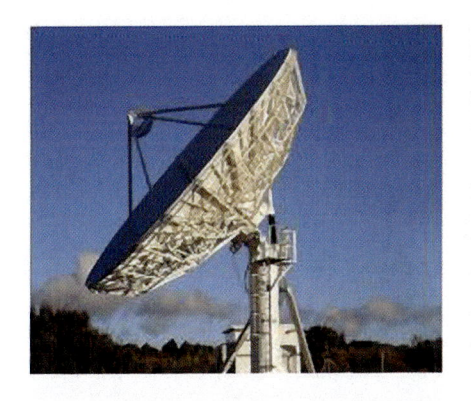

High-Capacity Satellite System

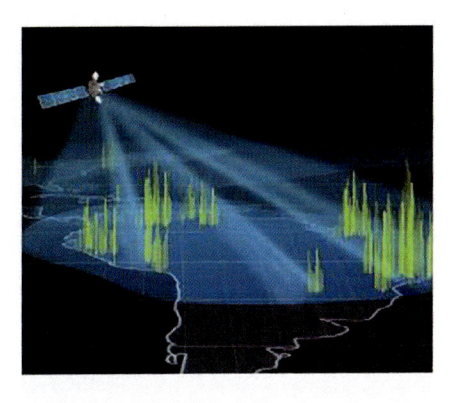

Ka-band Ground Systems

FROM VIASAT

In 1986, Mark Dankberg, Steve Hart, and Mark Miller founded Viasat Inc., a global communications company. By 1990, they delivered their first global communications test system, the VTS-3000 SATCOM. Founded in Georgia, the company moved its headquarters to Carlsbad, California in 1998, but maintains a metro Atlanta hub. Viasat has been named to *Defense News* Top 100 four times, *Space News* Top 50 five times, and *Forbes Magazine* 200 Best Small Companies six times. When the President of the United States tweets from *Air Force One,* he uses the same technology developed by VIASAT that enables everyday passengers to stream movies and check email on their personal computers inflight on a commercial aircraft. There are several layers of additional security for Air Force One, but the technology is the same. Here is a shortlist of 2019 accomplishments copied from VIASAT's website:

- Viasat signed contracts for the launch of its three Viasat-3 satellites with Arianespace, SpaceX and United Launch Alliance. The first of the trio is expected to launch in 2021.

- Viasat gained FAA approval to install its Ka-band in-flight connectivity system on super-midsize cabin business jets.

- Viasat contracted to deliver and test the first-ever Link 16-capable LEO spacecraft, intended to enhance communications for U.S. and allied military forces across the global battlespace.

- *Fortune* ranks Viasat number 12 on its 'Change the World' list for making a positive social impact through its core business activities.

- Viasat was named Global Satellite Business of the Year at Euroconsult's 2019 Awards for Excellence in Satellite Communications.

- Viasat announced its Real-Time Earth (RTE) service that provided ground station service support (from two of its U.S. ground stations: Georgia and Hawaii) to General Atomics Electromagnetic Systems' (GA-EMS) Orbital Test Bed (OTB) satellite.

Viasat's awards and recognitions include those from Business 2.0, *Via Satellite Magazine, Washington Technology,*

CHAPTER 10

97

Right: Photo from SouthWire Automation

American Institute of Aeronautics and Astronautics (AIAA), World Technology Network, *Guinness World Records*, *Popular Science*, Society of Satellite Professionals International (SSPI), Institution of Engineering and Technology, Defense Security Service for Counterintelligence, U.S. Green Building Council (USGBC), *Washington Technology*, and others.

SOUTHWIRE

Family-owned Southwire is a global company based in Carrollton, Georgia. The company's roots trace to Roy Richard's project "to erect power poles with the ultimate purpose of bringing electric lights to his grandmother's home." (Southwire)

Richard's new company "strung 3,500 miles of cable, becoming the nation's second-largest Rural Electrification ACT (REA) contractor" in its first twenty-six months of operation (Southwire). Soon after this accomplishment, Richards served the United States in World War II and returned home to find that most of the power poles his company had erected pre-war stood without wire because of shortages. In 1950, he led Richards & Associates (founded in 1937) into making wire as Southwire. Within two years, Southwire doubled in size, and had "shipped 5 million pounds of wire." (Southwire)

The company is now a leading global manufacturer. Eventually, Southwire "pioneered work in the development of next-generation power lines, also known as superconductivity. Working with the U.S. Department of Energy, Oak Ridge National Laboratory, and other industrial partners, Southwire developed superconductor power cable technology and introduced the first real-world application of superconductors in February 2000." (Southwire)

Kathleen Edge, Executive Vice President of Operations for Southwire, was a keynote for the Georgia Manufacturing Alliance 2016 Summit. She spoke from a Human Resources perspective concerning shifts in demographics, and how manufacturing will change to meet those shifts. Southwire sees their success as a product of learning from others, and therefore, they focus on giving back to others. Edge said, "It's not about the product we make, which is wire and cable to bring power to people's lives, it's about how we go about making the product. It's about people." The company's Human Resources goals are to build organizational capability by "leading with emotional intelligence, shaping culture for adaptability, and developing individual potential through performance management, career pathways, and succession planning." (Edge)

Southwire also supports an educational retention plan which helps students finish twelve years of education: "By providing our community's students with classroom instruction, on-the-job training, key work/life skills, mentoring, and employment opportunities, we're helping them stay in school, graduate, and go on to become successful, productive members of the workforce – ensuring those real-world skills translate into real-life success. It's hope. It's experience. And it's working." (Southwire)

Southwire, and other companies who now focus on training, are helping to bridge the skill gap created by shifting demographics.

NANOTECHNOLOGY

According to The *National Nanotechnology Initiative*, "Nanoscience and nanotechnology are the study and application of extremely small things and can be used across all the other science fields, such as chemistry, biology, physics, materials science, and engineering." (What is Nanotechnology)

Modern nanotechnology began in 1981 when scientists developed a tunneling microscope that allows the study of individual atoms, but concepts concerning nanotechnology began with physicist Richard Feynman in 1959. Professor Norio Taniguchi later coined the term *nanotechnology* and used the manipulation of atoms and molecules to develop ultraprecision machining. The *National Nanotechnology Initiative* states that "there are 25,400,000 nanometers in an inch, a sheet of newspaper is about 100,000 nanometers thick, and that, on a comparative scale, if a marble were a nanometer, then one meter would be the size of the Earth." The *National Nanotechnology Initiative* goes on to say that, "Today›s scientists and engineers are finding a wide variety of ways to deliberately make materials at nanoscale to take advantage of their enhanced properties such as higher strength, lighter weight, increased control of light spectrum, and greater chemical reactivity than their larger-scale counterparts." (What is Nanotechnology)

"Nanotechnology in Georgia – Companies, Research, and Degree Programs" lists "six companies in Georgia with a nanotechnology focus":

- Cabice Nanotechnologies develops innovative materials solutions that produce substantial value in electronic device markets including LEDs, high power computers, mobile devices, aerospace, and defense.

- Class One Equipment specializes in buying and selling high quality reconditioned process, metrology, assembly, test equipment to the semiconductor and nanotechnologies industries.

- Micromeritics provides a complete line of scientific instruments and laboratory equipment targeted exclusively for areas of application and research involving particle science and particle technology, including nanoscience.

- nGimat Co. manufactures engineered nanomaterials in nanopowders, thin-film coatings, and devices.

- Sila Nanotechnologies Inc. was founded in 2011 by a team of Silicon Valley entrepreneurs in collaboration with the Georgia Institute of Technology to revolutionize portable energy storage. They plan to create batteries that are lighter, smaller, and cheaper than today's state of the art lithium-ion technology.

- MVA Scientific Consultants, an analytical microscopy laboratory that provides nanomaterial characterization to raw material manufacturers and end-product users.

Non-commercial nanotechnology organizations in Georgia, according to "Nanotechnology in Georgia – Companies, Research, and Degree Programs," include Genetically Engineered Materials and Micro/Nano Devices, a MURI project at Georgia Institute of Technology focused on a revolutionary new paradigm for fabricating micro/nanodevices: the synergistic use of genetic engineering, biological replication, and shape-preserving chemical conversion to generate enormous numbers of identical Genetically-Engineered Micro/nanodevices (GEMs) with tailored 3-D shapes, fine (meso-to-nanoscale) features, and chemistries.

TECHNOLOGY ON A GEORGIA AIR FORCE BASE

Georgia's strategic location made her a military outpost from pre-colonial days. Here's an example of what the future holds: "Warner Robins Air Logistics Complex performs depot-level maintenance and repairs on a wide variety of Air Force equipment and weapons systems, including the C-5 Galaxy, C-130 Hercules, F-15 Strike Eagle, several Special Operations Forces aircraft, and the Predator and Reaper." (Robins Air Force Base, Georgia Fact Sheet)

It was natural, then, for Robins to perform maintenance on a new aircraft. Each task completed can lead to a new mission for the base, so when a Global Hawk drone landed at Robins Air Force Base on May 24, 2017, a first for any Air Force Air Logistics Complex, Robins' aircraft maintenance staff repainted the drone. In "Robins Air Force Base to Integrate Drones in Everyday Operations," Macon's 13WMAZ reported that "drones will help emergency response, law enforcement, and civil engineering on the base." (Hammond)

This technology will be widely used on military bases. Officials urge the public to know FAA rules and to obtain a Part 107 license if they plan to operate drones

Manufacturing Success in Georgia

commercially. What does the future hold? It holds a "B4UFly" app, and rules about flying drones over stadiums, public events, emergencies, and airfields.

Also, in 2020, "Warner Robins Air Logistics Complex shared plans for a new software engineering facility" that will employ one hundred fifty people: According to a press release, the project is a partnership between the Houston County Board of Commissioners, the Houston County Development Authority, the Houston County Board of Education, and the WR-ALC (Burse). It will boast a modern "Silicon Valley" style software lab. On June 12, 2020, the 52nd Combat Communications Squadron of Robins Air Force Base "launched their new Flexible Communications Package. The system can provide phone and internet service, in addition to access to the Air Force's network, to over 1,000 people from any location." (Drake) Welcome to the future.

GEORGIA'S TECHNOLOGY CORRIDORS

The Georgia Bioscience Joint Development Authority decided to "broaden the reach of interest for Georgia's Innovation Corridor from the original single focus on attracting bioscience companies, to encompass a wider range of potential future development." (Georgia Highway 316)

The route connects Atlanta to Athens and involves Athens-Clarke, Barrow, Oconee, and Gwinnett counties. It is the "first public body formed to drive and coordinate development in the GA 316 corridor to bring high-tech, high-paying jobs along the University Parkway, in a model based on North Carolina's Research Triangle." (Georgia Highway 316)

Georgia's High-Tech Corridor runs from Dublin toward McRae on Highway 441 and from Perry to Brunswick on 341. The Georgia General Assembly also designated SR 10/US 78 as the Technology Corridor to connect Augusta, with its Medical College of Georgia, and Athens, with the University of Georgia. This is the same legislation that designated highways 441 and 341 as the High-Tech Corridor. The establishment of these corridors shows that education fuels technology, and technology fuels Georgia's future. Colleges and their extension campuses located along Georgia's technology corridors, became more important during the 2020 COVID-19 Pandemic restrictions. Colleges and libraries, which have provided classes, computers, and the training to compete in a high-tech environment for years, proved their worth when university and college extensions moved exclusively to remote and online learning. Additionally, loss of manufacturing jobs in rural Georgia also increased a need for technically trained workers to operate in face-to-face or remote situations. Georgia's colleges also serve dual enrollment students who attend both high school and college or technical school simultaneously, and a growing number of non-traditional students (those over twenty-five years of age) use the campuses located along Georgia's technology corridors.

GEORGIA TECH

The "College of Management at the Georgia Institute of Technology (Georgia Tech) in Atlanta combines the principles of traditional business education with the dynamics of managing the constant innovation and worldwide reach of high technology. One executive program allows working professionals to earn a Master of Science in the management of technology. With an emphasis on technical innovations, entrepreneurship, and strategic planning, this degree has been dubbed by the college as 'the MBA for the age of technology.' The second program is the global executive MBA, which highlights issues related to international business and technology and includes four overseas residencies." (Carabello)

The Georgia Institute of Technology, or Georgia Tech, campus occupies four hundred fifty acres in Atlanta, and operates campuses in Savannah Georgia, France, and Singapore. The university "provides a broad technological education to more than 16,000 undergraduate and graduate students, and conducts a $300 million-per-year research program on the cutting edge of engineering, the sciences, computing, and many other disciplines." (Edwards and Toon) According to the *New Georgia Encyclopedia*, "In 2002 Georgia Tech received 40 patents and filed at least 188 invention, software, and copyright disclosures. More than two dozen inventions were licensed, demonstrating the commercial value of the innovations produced by Georgia Tech's research program."

GEORGIA RESEARCH ALLIANCE

Then there is always the need to connect academic advances to real-world applications. Georgia Research Alliance, a private non-profit based in Atlanta, works to partner "Georgia's business community, research universities, and state government. Its mission is to turn university research and development into economic gains for the state." (Robichaud)

By 2004, the Georgia Research Alliance brought "$2 billion in federal and private funding to Georgia, have helped to generate some ninety new companies based on university research and development, and have helped to create nearly 4,000 new high-tech jobs." (Robichaud)

SOFTWEAR

Technological advances affect the assembly line and the bottom line in Georgia manufacturing. One company that does this well is SoftWear. SoftWear uses advanced computer-assisted design software in the sewing industries. It creates "autonomous sewn good work lines for Home Goods, Footwear & Apparel. The Atlanta-based machine vision and robotics startup spun out of Georgia Tech after 7 years of research and development working on projects with DARPA and the WALMART Foundation. SoftWear's fully autonomous SEWBOT allows manufacturers to SEWLOCAL, moving their supply chains closer to the customer while creating higher quality products at a lower cost." (SoftWear)

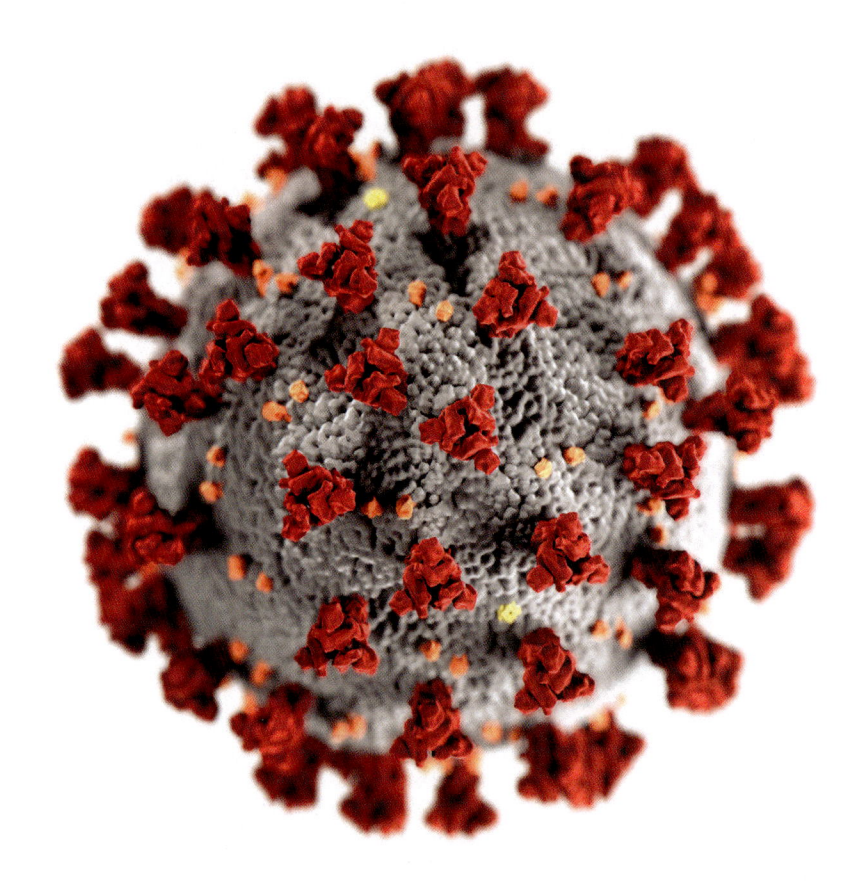

CHAPTER 11

COVID-19

The entire world has been impacted by the Coronavirus pandemic. Georgia Manufacturing was not immune to the devastation. We invited three members of GMA to add their thoughts to this book so that you could see the resilience and resolve.

LD DeKatch –FastSigns Snellville, Georgia

NECESSITY IS THE MOTHER OF INVENTION

I remember that saying from childhood while watching the *Schoolhouse Rock!* commercials. Since March of 2020, nothing has rung truer for our small manufacturing business.

COVID-19 created an environment of anxiety for many companies. The sad fact was that even though some companies would be able to adapt and stay open, there would be others that would have to close their doors forever. We certainly had feelings of anxiety over not being able to weather the storm, especially with so many of our customers having to shut their doors due to the "Shelter-In-Place" orders.

Being a sign company, we were one of the fortunate businesses to be considered "essential". But with so many of our clients not having that same luxury, we were at a

Manufacturing Success in Georgia

loss as to how and who we would be able to service. There were so many uncertainties, and we were just one small business in an entire nation treading in uncharted waters.

FASTSIGNS Snellville sat down with our small staff to discuss our game plan moving forward. Not only did we want to keep the business open, but we also wanted to keep ourselves, our families, and our customers safe. We were blessed to be part of a franchise whose corporate headquarters immediately started a task force to help all of its over seven hundred locations throughout the world. This mass collaboration assisted in figuring out how to help our communities during these unsettling times, and keep our businesses going.

We have always been community-oriented. So, our game plan was to look to the needs of those around us. We reached out to our local hospitals to see how we could help. With materials we already had in stock and equipment that was ready to be used, instead of making signs, we started producing face shields and intubation boxes. One of the owners jumped on her sewing machine to provide masks to our local healthcare facilities. Within a couple weeks, we started to see the needs of other "essential" businesses, and began to provide various countertop shields and signage to communicate new protocol and guidelines to their customers and employees.

As time passed, more businesses began to reopen, and we even started to see new businesses popping up in our community. The framework we had been living in just four short months before, was forever changed. The products that we are offering now, in addition to signage, were so different from the products we had been offering over the past seven years. Products we never dreamt of producing or ever thought would be needed were now accounting for so much of our business.

Although there seemed to be a rift happening across the country over the current situation, on a local level, the manufacturing community seemed to bind together. The Georgia Manufacturing Alliance offered a platform for us to gather resources and materials, share best practices and ideas, and even foster hope in each other during these turbulent times. It was nothing short of inspirational to see other companies filling the niches around them in new ways to keep our economy going. The transparency between manufacturers, their owners, and employees have created a bond that only difficult times can produce. As we have all learned, change is not without growing pains and resiliency is superior to resistance.

Joe Paolini - Bobby Dodd Institute – Atlanta, Georgia

The Covid-19 pandemic may end up being the greatest leadership challenge that any of us will ever face. It has changed the way we lead our organizations, how we lead our families and friends, and how we navigate our day to day lives. From how Chick-Fil-A gets ordered, to how our children attend school, we are experiencing constant change necessitating adjustments. As business leaders, we have been put in a position of navigating uncharted waters while trying to protect the jobs, livelihoods, and health of those around us. It is an unenviable position, but it is one in which greatness thrives. The lessons we learn from both our victories and our shortcomings throughout the Covid-19 experience will continue to shape our organizations for years to come.

The Georgia manufacturing community, and the leadership around it, has stepped up to the challenge of engaging and being a guiding light through this difficult time. Safety measures have been reinvented, communication has increased, and organizations have more fully embraced technology. In the State of Georgia, the manufacturing community has changed for the better since March 2020. Great innovation has occurred on every level; from front line workers to the board room, and it has strengthened our State and manufacturing community. We have embraced this collectively together and have set a model for the rest of the nation to follow.

Bobby Dodd Institute is a mission-minded nonprofit located in Atlanta. Our organization seeks to empower people with differing abilities to maximize their potential by securing economic self-sufficiency, independence, and inclusion within their communities. The partnerships that we have been able to develop during this time will have lasting positive impacts on the people with differing abilities community. Key executives from organizations such as GMA, J&S Chemical, and Grenzebach have engaged BDI to develop work, and connections, that have proven valuable to the community that we serve. During Covid-19, BDI has been able to increase business in our warehouse, facility management services, and we even started bottling hand sanitizer. All of this directly benefits the differing abilities community, by providing much needed job opportunities, and reflects the resiliency within the Georgia manufacturing community.

As we look to the future, the Georgia manufacturing community will continue to lead the way on both a state and national stage. Through strong leadership, hard work, and thoughtful planning; Bobby Dodd Institute is excited for the future, and proud of its involvement with Georgia manufacturing.

ED BISHOP – MURRAY PLASTIC – GAINESVILLE, GEORGIA

"'Twas the year of the Covid and all through the sales, not a customer's door opened, nor a call be returned. So, considering my options to flourish or fail, I considered a team leading through it well!"

PERSONAL GROWTH THROUGH COVID

My career at Murray Plastics started in 1992, pausing from 2015 to 2020 to explore and increase my understanding of the plastics industry. When the pandemic hit, I had an opportunity to reevaluate my strengths and possibly return to Murray Plastics.

What would be enjoyable and where could I contribute the most? Jason Moss was a great wing-man helping me through the process. I wanted to go where I could make a difference with a team, I knew was making a difference.

May 1st began my move from sales to operations at Murray Plastics. The transition in the time of the unknown was without concern as they made me aware of the processes that were put in place to ensure everyone in the workplace was safe and distanced per local requirements.

Personal Lessons Learned:

- Flexibility and the ability to adapt and change is key to leading through these challenging times.
- I needed to avoid my tendency to be rigid in my thinking and be open to new ideas and opportunities. This can also be a challenge to those people or companies that are not adept to change.
- You always need someone in your life that is willing to help you grow to the best of your abilities no matter what.

BUSINESS SUCCESS STORY:

During the pandemic year of 2020, Murray Plastics flourished. With a vision for the future, we purchased two new molds for an existing product line and added a robot. The robot allowed Murray Plastics to automate five different Tayloreel products while integrating the process of dipping the parts in an anti-static solution, which increased the efficiencies tremendously.

This improvement allowed us to train operators for new job functions which included material handling, inspecting, and packaging products. We also purchased a new thermolator and material dryer to help us with our custom injection molding customers. These purchases also provided our suppliers with a boost to maintain their product sales in a tough economy.

I hope you find my personal success story, or our company's progress through this tough environment, encouraging. Always keep looking for new opportunities, as they may come from directions you least expect them, and be willing to consider new options to move forward.

"A team that leads through challenging times is a team that is worth learning from and growing with!"

CHAPTER 12

SIGN-OFF

So, the story ends as it begins with Manufacturing Success in Georgia. Our state started with natural resources, a diverse and productive society, crafters who moved their skills to manufacturing, academics who developed technology, and manufacturers who advance productivity using that technology. Georgia's future is as bright, creative, varied, and as productive as her people.

As Manufacturing in Georgia is polished and headed for publication in 2020, Georgia is ranked as having the seventh-lowest unemployment rate in the country. Contributing factors to this success include political leaders working tirelessly in conjunction with business leaders to find common-sense solutions to keep hard-working Georgians employed. Governor Brian Kemp has maintained his focus on "Protecting the lives and livelihoods of every Georgian," and the results speak for themselves.

The rebound of manufacturing in Georgia is leading the way for the economic recovery in our state and nation. Although many businesses were unable to weather the impact of 2020's COVID-19 pandemic restrictions, most companies did and they are experiencing growth. They did this by experimenting with new product options, exploring new markets, and restructuring the workplace to improve efficiency. It's exciting to look back on Georgia's rich manufacturing history and even more exciting to what the future holds.

Sharing The Heritage

Historical profiles of businesses and individuals that have contributed to the development and continued Manufacturing Success in Georgia

    Gulfstream 110

    KIA..116

    Daniel Defense 124

    Southwire...126

    Pye-Barker..129

    American Metal Craft..132

    KaMin 133

    DeNyse Sign 134

Gulfstream Aerospace Corporation

Gulfstream Aerospace Corporation is a wholly-owned subsidiary of General Dynamics, which designs, develops, manufactures, markets, services and supports the world's most technologically advanced business-jet aircraft. The company has produced more than 3,200 aircraft for customers around the world since 1958. To meet the diverse transportation needs of the future, Gulfstream offers a comprehensive fleet of aircraft, including the super-midsize Gulfstream G280™, the award-winning Gulfstream G650™, the high-performing Gulfstream G650ER™ and an all-new aircraft family, the clean-sheet Gulfstream G500™, Gulfstream G600™ and new industry flagship, the Gulfstream G700™.

All aircraft are backed by Gulfstream's Customer Support network and its worldwide team. Gulfstream's Mission Statement guides the company in "Creating and Delivering the World's Finest Aviation Experience."

The history of Gulfstream Aerospace begins with Grumman Aircraft Engineering Company, which was founded December 6, 1929. That company renamed itself at Grumman Aircraft Engineering Corporation in 1966 and then Grumman American Aviation Corporation in 1973. It became a subsidiary of American Jet Industries Inc., a California company owned by Allen Paulson, in September 1978 and the name was changed to Gulfstream American Corp. The name

Manufacturing Success in Georgia

was officially changed in November 1982 to Gulfstream Aerospace Corp.

Aviation pioneers Leroy (Roy) Randle Grumman, along with friends, A.P. Loening, Grover Loening, E. Clinton Towl and Edwin W. Poor, launched the Grumman Aircraft Engineering Company from a rented garage in Baldwin, New York, on December 6, 1929. With their savings and careers at risk, this entrepreneurial team worked hard to achieve their vision and would go on to win wartime contracts to create legendary combat aircraft like the Hellcat, A-6 Intruder and F-14 Tomcat. After World War II, Roy Grumman proposed the development of a purpose-built business aircraft—he said he felt inspired by the belief that aviation could fuel business growth. Thirteen years later, Grumman introduced the Gulfstream I™—the world's first purpose-built business aircraft. The Gulfstream I, named for the swift, powerful and reliable Gulf Stream ocean current along the U.S. eastern coastline, made its first flight on August 14, 1958, and entered service one year later. The first-of-its-kind aircraft was designed with passenger comfort in mind and featured the now signature Gulfstream oval windows. In 1966, Grumman—now Grumman Aircraft Engineering Corp.—split aircraft production into two divisions, civil and military, to provide better efficiency. The company acquired 110 acres at Travis Field in Savannah, Georgia, in April of that same year. Executives cited a ready supply of skilled labor, a temperate climate perfect for year-round flight-testing, well-developed infrastructure and both training and innovation as key motivators for moving business-aircraft operations to Savannah. The agreement with local leaders stated the new plant had to provide employment for at least 500 people. On September 29, 1967, Grumman officially moved operations to Savannah. But before the company opened their new location in Savannah, Grumman introduced the world to the Gulfstream GII™ with its first flight on October 2, 1966. Once operations began in Savannah, the 100-person GII

SHARING THE HERITAGE

team, 90 percent of them local, went on to grow to 1,700 in a few years. The GII would go on to set record after record and ushered in the jet age as the first business aircraft to connect Europe and the U.S. in a single flight on May 4, 1968. And five years later, two GIIs were modified to serve as training aircraft for the NASA (National Aeronautics and Space Administration, U.S.A.) Shuttle program, with astronauts using the jets to practice approach and landing maneuvers.

In October of 1969, Gulfstream announced a $1 million expansion of the Savannah plant, and in October of 1974, more plans for expansion come through as well as 200 new jobs. On December 2, 1979, The Gulfstream III™ made its first flight. With a new wing design and the addition of winglets, the aircraft stretched the limits of its predecessor and, in November 1983, would distinguish itself as the first business aircraft to fly over both poles. As Gulfstream maintained a global focus and stratospheric ambitions, the company introduced the Gulfstream GIV™ and the aircraft made its first flight on September 19, 1985. The GIV revolutionized business aviation with its intercontinental range, speed and advanced cockpit technology, and the GIV family of aircraft, which includes the GIV, GIV-SP™, G400™ and G450™, went on to set more than 90 internationally recognized aviation records. Gulfstream would go on to sell and deliver more than 800 aircraft, making the GIV family Gulfstream's best-selling aircraft. In 1996, Gulfstream opened a 200,000-square-foot service center in Savannah, making it the largest for corporate aircraft in North America and the following year Gulfstream established another first by simultaneously manufacturing more than one model with the Gulfstream GIV-SP and the GV™. The large-cabin GV made its first flight on November 28, 1995, and went on to win the prestigious Robert J. Collier Trophy for advanced design and manufacturing techniques in May 1997.

On July 30, 1999, defense giant General Dynamics purchased Gulfstream Aerospace Corp. for US$5.3 billion and made research and development a priority. They would also accelerate Gulfstream's entry into the midsize aircraft market with

Manufacturing Success in Georgia

the acquisition of Galaxy Aerospace in 2001. With that purchase, Gulfstream gained the Astra SPX (rebranded Gulfstream 100™) and the Galaxy (rebranded Gulfstream G200™).

Gulfstream's Quiet Spike went supersonic on October 23, 2006.

On January 28, 2008 Gulfstream debuted its Synthetic Vision-Primary Flight Display system.

On May 7, 2002, Gulfstream launched its Airborne Product Support service program, and on May 16, 2011, Gulfstream introduced Gulfstream FAST™, its Field and Airborne Support Teams.

Gulfstream Aerospace Corporation operates in Savannah, Georgia; Appleton, Wisconsin; Beijing, China; Brunswick, Georgia; Dallas, Texas; Baja California, Mexico; Lincoln, Long Beach, and Van Nuys, California; Farnborough and Luton, United Kingdom; Palm Beach, Florida; St. Louis, Missouri; and Westfield, Massachusetts; maintaining Sales and Design centers in London; United Kingdom; Manhattan, New York.; Dallas, Texas; Appleton, Wisconsin; and Long Beach, California.

In Georgia, Gulfstream employs approximately 9,300 people. Worldwide, the employee headcount has increased since 2010, from approximately, 9,000 employees to nearly 15,000. The company headquarters is in Savannah, Georgia. Gulfstream's customer base is primarily publicly and privately held corporations.

In 2019, Gulfstream's international community investments included more than 130 nonprofits supported around the globe, more than 1,100 Student Leadership graduates, and a $1.75 million United Way donation from a combination of employee and company donations. Gulfstream completed several community

SHARING THE HERITAGE

investment initiatives at their various locations including a project to deliver 16,000 pounds of supplies to the Bahamas after Hurricane Dorian.

Gulfstream leads the business aviation industry in using certified sustainable aviation fuel (SAF). The sustainability strategy originated with a mandate from the company's senior leadership for Gulfstream and its employees to act as stewards of the environment for their communities. Gulfstream is also the first business jet manufacturer to use a dedicated supply of SAF. In 2019, the company approached a milestone of one million nautical miles flown on SAF and to date has saved more than 1,700 metric tons of carbon dioxide as they continue to build aircraft that are fuel-efficient by design.

In Georgia, Gulfstream partners with Childhood Obesity Prevention and Education (COPE), the National Museum of the Mighty Eighth Air Force, the Salvation Army, Savannah Telfair Museum, Live Oak Public Libraries, Chatham-Savannah Citizen Advocacy, America's Second Harvest Food Bank, Boys and Girls Club, Hospice Savannah Foundation, Union Mission, United Way of the Coastal Empire, United Way of Coastal Georgia, Brunswick-Golden Isles Chamber of Commerce, Communities in Schools of Glynn County, and Leadership Glynn to improve communities. Gulfstream also focuses on education by partnering with the Student Leadership Program (SLP), Savannah-Chatham County Public School System, Golden Isles Career Academy—In partnership with the Glynn County School System, Aviation Manufacturing and Service Program at Groves High School, and forty businesses, 600 students, and 120 volunteer advisors annually. Other partnerships include State of Georgia Youth Apprenticeship—Internship program

Manufacturing Success in Georgia

for public high school students that exposes them to STEM careers while they gain real-world work experience-op and intern program with area colleges, Georgia Tech VET2 Program, which is an Internship program with active-duty military, Savannah Technical College, and holds Aviation Career Days—Middle schools in Glynn, McIntosh, Brantley and Camden counties.

Gulfstream Aerospace Corporation is a leading manufacturer of the world's most advanced business aircraft, with almost 15,000 employees worldwide. Approximately twenty-five percent of the company's U.S. employees are veterans. Headquartered in Savannah, Georgia, United States with facilities in fourteen major locations across three continents, Gulfstream has been a wholly owned subsidiary of General Dynamics since 1999. For more, visit gulfstream.com.

The KMMG Story

The massive automobile manufacturing facilities of Kia Motors Manufacturing Georgia (KMMG), occupy a 1.3-mile stretch of real estate adjacent to I-85 near the Chattahoochee River that delineates the borders of Georgia and Alabama. A water tower boasting a Kia brand logo accents the site as a landmark, standing tall as a symbol of recovery and progress for the small town of West Point, Ga. that KMMG calls home.

At the turn of the 21st Century, the 3,400 citizens of West Point witnessed a mass exodus of the textile industry as local mills were shuttered and equipment was relocated around the globe, leaving thousands in the area unemployed. While families with generations of ties to the southwest corner of Troup County began to consider relocation to areas with better job possibilities, a sign of hope swept through the community, stirring the air with optimism and anticipation of a brighter future.

In March 2006, officials from Kia Motors joined then Governor Sonny Perdue in the announcement of Kia's decision to construct its first U.S. operation, a $1 billion, state-of-the- art manufacturing facility, to produce new generations of Kia products sold in North America. The announcement was the culmination of months of study and planning with local, county and state officials with a common goal of sourcing a major automotive manufacturing operation in Georgia.

Shortly thereafter, Chairman Mung-koo Chung hosted a groundbreaking ceremony and construction equipment began to clear the site that would eventually employ over 5,000 KMMG Team Members, on-site suppliers and contractors. Coordinated projects with the Georgia's Department of Economic Development and Department of Transportation, along with the Georgia Ports Authority and other state agencies were soon underway, providing the necessary infrastructure to support KMMG's ability to move materials and products through its facility.

Manufacturing Success in Georgia

With site preparation efforts in full stride, KMMG and Georgia's workforce development agency, Quick Start, celebrated the opening of the Kia-Georgia Training Center (KGTC). A model for workforce training programs, Georgia Quick Start facilitated the first online application process in the state and has processed over 125,000 applications for Kia jobs…over 43,000 accepted within the first 30 days. The KGTC provided an advanced industrial training program with emphasis on safety, quality and standardization which continues to play a vital role in KMMG's operations.

The KMMG plan for success was built on the company's Core Values of Customer, Challenge, Collaboration, People and Globality… principles upon which its operational model, The Kia Way was based. Supported by a foundation of mutual trust, The Kia Way fosters an organizational culture that promotes a One System, One Team mindset centered on standardized processes and continuous improvement in all facets of its operation.

KMMG Team Members are introduced to The Kia Way from the very beginning stages of the company's New Hire Orientation, which is followed by a progressive 3-step training program that emphasizes the importance of following established standards in safety and quality in all KMMG processes. As they gain experience and proficiency in their assigned processes, KMMG Team Members are encouraged to participate in group and cross-functional activities to explore improvement opportunities within the operation.

Months of preparation, training and anticipation gave way to success on November. 16, 2009, as KMMG celebrated the official launch of its first model, the 2011 Kia Sorento. A new generation for the model, the Sorento set higher standards and expectations in

SHARING THE HERITAGE

design, quality and safety for the Kia brand and put KMMG on the path to becoming a world class automotive operation.

KMMG's launch of its first product also launched a growth plan in operational capacity and U.S. market share. In less than three years, KMMG was producing three different models on the same lines with an industry-leading three shift operation. The 2011 launch of the Kia Optima increased the factory's annual capacity to over 300,000 units per year, while the popularity of KMMG vehicles continued to soar.

A $100 million expansion to the site was completed in 2012 to increase annual production capacity to 360,000. The popularity of KMMG products pushed the facility to higher levels in 2016, with the production total topping 371,000. KMMG produced over three million vehicles in less than ten years of operation, accounting for over 40 percent of the total U.S. sales for the Kia brand. The company exports to Canada, Mexico, Central and South American countries, as well as countries in the Middle East.

KMMG's production system is efficiently driven by a synchronized and disciplined "Just in Time, Just in Sequence" logistics system that delivers modules and assembly parts from local suppliers to the designed process area just as they are needed for assembly to KMMG vehicles. The KMMG supplier base, located along the I-85 corridor in West Georgia and Eastern Alabama and have created over 13,000 additional jobs in the area.

Rolls of coiled steel are delivered into KMMG's Stamping Shop where they are unfurled and cut into a variety of lengths and geometric patterns called "blanks" and staged for stamping. Two 5400-ton presses are tasked with stamping the blanks into panels that form the bodies of KMMG products. Panels to build hoods, doors and fenders flow from the stamping presses every five seconds and are prepared for the assembly process. KMMG Stamping Team Members, tasked with maintaining the battery of enormous dies that are used to stamp each part, are among the best in the industry. Their efficiency and accuracy in die setting enables them to perform a complete four-stage die change in less than six minutes, a global benchmark for stamping equipment of its size.

The assembly process begins in

Manufacturing Success in Georgia

the KMMG Body Shop, where every product receives its identity. The Vehicle Identification Number or VIN assigned to each unit begins the tracking for processing through the plant and initiates orders for assembly parts needed from the supply base. Over 300 robots equipped with sealing tools, welders and part handlers combine to assemble the body structure and closures across the shop with dimensional accuracy tolerances of less than one millimeter. Welding robots complete over 2,000 welds to assemble the metal structure of each vehicle, providing the strength and rigidity necessary to achieve the highest ratings in safety standards and the overall performance of the vehicle.

Once the body's structure is completed, it is transported through the 6.9 miles of conveyors that route through KMMG's Paint Shop. An 11-stage cleaning and conditioning process prepares the metal structure for an electro-deposition process, providing corrosion protection to every part of the body. Over 100 robots masterfully apply sealer, sound deadeners, and paint coatings with precision and consistency to every vehicle body. Paint Shop Team Members place a personal touch of perfection through careful inspections at each stage of the process to assure that every unit achieves the level of quality in appearance and color harmony.

KMMG's Assembly Shop transforms the painted bodies into world class quality vehicles that compete on a global scale. This series of parallel assembly conveyors line the massive production floor, moving vehicles through an orchestra of KMMG Team Members performing synchronous, sequential and progressive assembly processes to install hundreds of assembly parts and modules required for each product. Each job station consists of an established set of tasks to be completed by Team Members, based on the build requirements of each unit.

Ergonomically designed conveyor systems, tooling and adjustable job station equipment allows Team Members to focus their efforts on the process requirements and integrity of a very flexible operation. Quality checks are built into each step and validated through a variety of control systems and inspections by experts in Kia's rigid quality standards. At the end of the

SHARING THE HERITAGE

assembly process, Kia products roll off the line at rate of up to 70 vehicles per hour, where they are started and driven through the functional quality confirmation steps.

After the assembly process is completed, every KMMG product is driven through the 2.2-mile test track which consists of various road surfaces and driving evaluations, checking for possible issues detectable only while driving. The testing is finalized by routing each vehicle through the "shower test" which subjects the unit to a high-pressure rain simulation, checking for water leaks.

After all quality checks are conducted and confirmed, Kia products are routed to an on-site processing area that prepares them for shipping to their assigned destination. Approximately 60 percent of KMMG products are shipped by railroad from the facility's dedicated rail spur across the U.S., while the remainder is transported by truck, primarily to the southeastern region of the U.S.

The success of the KMMG team has been recognized throughout the spectrum of automotive critics and journalists. Products produced in the West Point facility have garnered Five-Star safety designations from the Insurance Institute of Highway Safety (IIHS), while quality and reliability publications have credited KMMG for leading the way in Kia's advancement in customer satisfaction and brand image.

KMMG's Sorento and Optima models have ranked at the top of their respective segments in the J.D. Power and Associates' Initial Quality Study results, with the Sorento placing first in its segment in 2015, 2017 and 2018. The consistent top-level rankings of KMMG products were key factors in the achievement of the Kia brand's recognition as the "Top Mass Market Brand" for five consecutive years by J.D. Power and Associates.

The addition of the Kia Telluride in 2019 marked the first KMMG launch of a totally new product designed specifically for the U.S. market in Kia's design studio in California. The new model presented an opportunity for the KMMG Team Members to demonstrate their ability to support a global market with a product built solely in the Georgia facility. The result was unprecedented, not only for

Manufacturing Success in Georgia

Kia, but for the entire U.S. market in the category of sport utility vehicles.

In its first year, the Telluride was awarded top rankings by Consumer Reports, Kelley Blue Book and Edmunds.com, while taking the "Triple Crown" in automotive journalism by winning top SUV awards from "Car and Driver," "Motor Trend" and the heralded "North American Utility Vehicle of the Year" award.

The growth in KMMG's operation has been mirrored by the economic recovery of the small railroad town it calls home. Shuttered buildings have reopened with a variety of new businesses, while riverfront projects are underway in West Point and neighboring communities, revitalizing enthusiasm of a community with a bright future.

KMMG's impact in West Georgia goes well beyond the jobs and economic recovery generated in the area with its investment of time and money into local communities. The company's Corporate Social Responsibility program provides a comprehensive approach to support the community, focusing on education, environment, diversity and inclusion and health and wellness efforts in the local area.

Through a partnership with the SAE Foundation, KMMG has sponsored "A World in Motion" programs for local county and city school systems to provide hands-on activities that focus on STEM (Science, Technology, Engineering and Mathematics) disciplines. The projects are provided to classrooms from kindergarten to middle school with customized training for the teachers and support by volunteers from the plant. Through the program, over 500 fifth grade students from participating schools form teams that compete in a state contest each year in Atlanta Local teams also participate in a national competition in Detroit each spring.

KMMG is a Charter Sponsor of the THINC College and Career Academy in Troup County, a model facility for the state of Georgia that provides high school students the opportunity to explore a variety of career fields. Additional partnerships and activities through the THINC Expeditions program has

SHARING THE HERITAGE

resulted in opportunities for THINC students to work inside KMMG's operations, nurturing the development of "real world" skill sets necessary for success in the workplace.

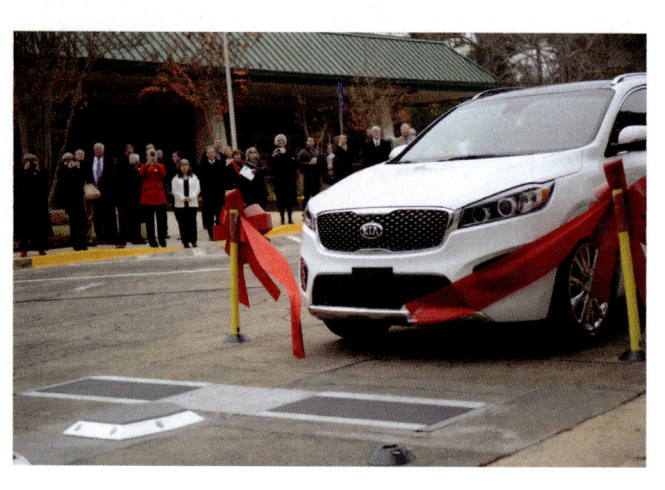

The company's workforce development initiatives have generated dozens of co-op programs for students in technical colleges and universities in Georgia and Alabama, while partnerships with the Technical College System of Georgia has resulted in specialized training for specific skill needs in various areas of KMMG's operations.

In its efforts of environmental stewardship, KMMG has partnered with organizations such as The Ray and The Georgia Conservancy to promote environmental awareness and the sustainability of natural resources. The company as conducted dozens of community service projects through which KMMG team members volunteer to support the protection and preservation of the area's natural resources, such as the West Point Lake and the Chattahoochee riverfront.

KMMG's efforts on health and wellness are highlighted by its sponsorship of an annual 5K race that is open to the public. Hundreds of KMMG Team Members and runners from the region meet each spring to participate in the competition, which emphasizes the importance of healthy habits and lifestyles. KMMG has also partnered with the West Georgia Health Foundation to provide free transportation of cancer patients to and from their medical treatment appointments as a part of its "Kia in the Community" initiative.

The community impact from KMMG's programs is accented by the involvement and participation of its Team Members. The Matching Gift program is a product of Team Members' financial donations to one or more of several community charities supporting the region. Additionally, KMMG's Team Members join to support the needs of the area through generous support in food drives, Back to School supplies, and "Toys for Tots" programs.

KMMG's rapid evolution into a world class operation with industry leading product quality and performance has

Manufacturing Success in Georgia

ignited the interest of industry analysts, news and entertainment media, as well as automotive enthusiasts across the nation. KMMG's operation has been featured in The History Channel's "Modern Marvels" series and The Discovery Channel-Canada, which highlighted the advanced manufacturing capabilities of the plant and the emphasis the operation places on quality and teamwork in its feature of the Optima launch in "The Birth of a Kia Optima."

In November 2019, Executive Vice Chairman Euisun Chung and the KMMG team celebrated the 10-year anniversary of the plant. Georgia Governor Brian Kemp, Congressman Drew Ferguson and representatives from various state agencies joined with local and county officials and guests to commemorate the event, highlighting the decade of success of the KMMG team.

In his address to the KMMG team and its honored guests, Executive Vice Chairman Chung noted the impact of evolving technologies on the automotive industry, noting the changes in product, how they are manufactured, and the way customers will use them in the future. Chung confirmed the importance of KMMG's role in the U.S. market and expressed confidence and commitment to the West Point facility and its team on the company's bright future.

In acknowledgement of its milestone anniversary, KMMG announced the beginning of its public tour program to allow customers, visitors and industry enthusiasts to learn more about the Kia brand, the KMMG story and tour the plant during operation. Tour requests may be made through KMMG's website, kmmgusa.com.

A decade after the announcement of Kia's arrival to Georgia, KMMG continues to thrive in its operations and growth, as well as in its impact on the community. Its story of success is lined with the spirit of determination of countless individuals challenged by the desolation of industry and obstacles of a changing world, working together with a "Can Do" mindset and a common goal to produce change in THEIR world, on THEIR terms.

SHARING THE HERITAGE

Daniel Defense

Located in Black Creek, Georgia, Daniel Defense is a family-owned, privately-held firearms manufacturer. In its brief twenty-year history, Daniel Defense, one of the most recognizable brands in the firearms world, has produced the world's finest AR15-style rifles, pistols, bolt action rifles, and accessories for civilian, law enforcement and military customers. Daniel Defense is centered on its commitment to the liberty of our country, the enthusiasm of its customers and employees, and the quality and accuracy of its products. The story of Daniel Defense begins with its founder, President and CEO Marty Daniel, who started the company in 2000, with the idea of creating custom accessories for his personal rifles. Since its inception, the company has worked to control every facet of production, and today makes nearly every component part it sells. This differentiates Daniel Defense from others in the industry who assemble rather than build their products. The process begins with Daniel Defense' design engineering team who extends boundaries and renders the status quo obsolete with a customer-centric approach to product design, asking the question, "What are features of this design that benefit the ones who will actually be using this product?" From there, the finest materials like ultra-high-strength stainless steel, aircraft-grade aluminum, carbon-fiber-reinforced polymers, and nickel super alloys are used. Daniel Defense also uses state-of-the art technology and robotics to manufacture its own parts. Barrels are made from proprietary steel and stainless-steel alloys on GFM Radial Cold Hammer Forging machines. Over 90 CNC machines precisely mill parts and components with exacting tolerances. The high-performance DDWAVE sound suppressors are 3D printed using a direct-metal laser-sintering

Manufacturing Success in Georgia

process. Once something is manufactured, the company exercises industry-leading quality-control measures and technology, like utilizing coordinating measuring machines, optical vision systems, and in-house designed specialty gauging to make sure every component meets or exceeds its demanding standards. Only then, do the products make it into a customer's hands. One of the first in the industry to use a cold hammer forging process to build the world's most accurate and durable barrels, and using its own in-house robotic Cerakote finishing line, Daniel Defense controls its own destiny to better serve consumers. This was only enhanced in 2017 when the company moved into its state-of-the-art 300,000 square foot manufacturing facility. By leveraging its design and manufacturing efficiencies, the company successfully provides consumers custom quality products worthy of their price. This attention to design and state-of-the-art manufacturing processes allows Daniel to provide life time guarantees for its products. Whether it's the first owner or fifth owner; Daniel stands behind its product. And, if customers have a problem, the Daniel Customer Service Team, American employees located in America, happily assist and make things right. At Daniel Defense, as long as someone backs one of our products, so do we.

SHARING THE HERITAGE

Southwire Company, LLC

Southwire Company, LLC is a leader in technology and innovation and an emerging influence in the industrial electrical space. One of North America's largest wire and cable producers, Southwire and its subsidiaries manufacture building wire and cable, metal-clad cable, utility products, portable and electronic cord products OEM wire products and engineered products. Southwire supplies assembled products, contractor equipment and hand tools. Southwire's entrepreneurial success began with the vision and drive of its founder, Roy Richards, Sr. Fresh out of the U.S. Army, Richards, a graduate of Georgia Tech, created a wire and cable manufacturing business to bring electricity to rural Carroll County, Georgia. Richards' strong personal impetus was simple: "My grandmother is eighty-five years old, and she has never had the pleasure of sitting under an electric light in her own house." Stymied by long delays in obtaining manufactured wire from other companies, Richards began producing wire with twelve employees and second-hand machinery in March 1950. From this modest beginning, Southwire has grown to international presence with nearly 7,000 employees. Expansion, both organically and through acquisition, extended Southwire's reach accordingly. As one of the leading manufacturers of wire and cable used in the transmission and distribution of electricity, Southwire delivers power to millions of people globally. Nearly one in two houses built in the United States contain the company's wire. More than one-half of the world's refined copper passes through one of its patented SCR® systems, and its products play key roles in other manufacturing applications. Southwire's driving force has been The People Behind the Power™. From its founder and leadership, continuing through the ranks of its loyal employees, the company's rich history illustrates their significant contributions. It began with company giants influencing the trajectory of Southwire's success. Roy Richards realized that he would have to train a work force for his new wire mill, and turned to his mentor, Maj. A.A. Case, a mechanical shop instructor at Georgia Tech, to set

Manufacturing Success in Georgia

up the new shop and help develop the crucial, skilled workforce. Richards saw Case's enthusiasm as "infectious" and vital to the company's start. Margaret Braswell, a childhood friend of Richards, saw, early on, his potential for success. A bookkeeper and secretary in the early days, she served as corporate secretary/treasurer, supervising the flow of millions of dollars over the years. Jim Griffin joined Southwire as its third salesman in 1953 and stayed for more than thirty years, thriving on its growth and saying he was "always learning something new." Pete Cofer, a young engineer fresh out of Georgia Tech, shepherded the difficult project of perfecting the Southwire Continuous Rod System (SCR), which revolutionized the industry, allowing for continuous casting of copper and aluminum rod. Southwire honored Cofer's invaluable contributions by naming its research and development center after him in 1992. Roy Richards, Sr. guided Southwire through decades of growth and innovation. His tenure included the invention of SCR technology and construction of the company's first building wire plant. In 1969, Southwire opened its Hawesville, Kentucky plant, negotiated the largest industrial revenue bond ($142 million) in Wall Street history, for construction of an aluminum smelter. In 1984, Roy Richards, Sr. was named "Copper Man of the Year." He passed away in 1985, a pivotal year for Southwire, and was eventually succeeded as CEO by his son, Roy Richards, Jr.

Under Roy, Jr.'s leadership, Southwire continued to expand its operations with the development of superconductivity next generation power lines and continued company growth. In 2001, Southwire turned to leadership outside of the Richards family, as Stu Thorn became President, and eventually CEO. The ensuing years reaffirmed the company's commitment to community and to innovation. In 2005, amid the devastation left from Hurricane Katrina, Southwire initiated Project GIFT®, Giving Inspiration for Tomorrow, which today involves more than a thousand company volunteers supporting local community projects. To help address the ever-increasing high school dropout rate, Southwire partnered with local school systems to create the 12 for Life® program, which inspires at-risk students to earn wages by working in a Southwire manufacturing facility while completing high school. The program has graduated and changed the lives of more than 2,900 students, some of whom have continued to work at Southwire or go on to further their education, enter the military, or pursue other occupations, while also helping improve the county's graduation rates. Throughout its history, a few underlying themes have driven the company forward: growth, innovation and community. These threads weave together in Southwire's 2007 formalized commitment to sustainability and are underscored in its mission to "work every day to discover, develop and distribute sustainable solutions that exceed the expectations of our stakeholders around the world." This commitment is led by five tenets: Growing Green, Living Well, Giving Back, Doing Right and Building Worth. Southwire continued these themes, introducing SIM Pull

SHARING THE HERITAGE

Solutions® in 2008, an entire line of products and services geared to make wire pulls easier for contractors. Proof Positive Copper®, which debuted in 2010, became Southwire's solution to copper theft in the industry. And, in 2013, the company introduced a line of hand tools, meters and testers, a business that continues to grow and influence the industry, organically and through acquisition, by introducing innovative tools, components and assembled solutions. In 2016, Rich Stinson was named President and CEO. Under Stinson, the company focuses on its goal to remain generationally sustainable, with three strategic goals to Build Organizational Capability, Drive Operational Excellence and Accelerate Growth. Recent acquisitions include United Copper Industries, Sumner Manufacturing, DCN Cables, ProBuilt Lighting, Garvin Industries, Madison Electric and Construction Electrical Products. Additionally, to promote hands-on-learning and education for contractors, distributors and apprentices, Southwire opened its Thorn Customer Solutions Center in 2017, a state-of-the-art training center. Proudly calling Carrollton, Georgia headquarters, Southwire invites you to learn more at www.southwire.com.

Pye-Barker Engineered Solutions

The story of Pye-Barker Engineered Solutions begins with the vision and drive of its founders. It all started back in the mid-1930s, with a couple off fellow Georgia Tech graduates, John Pye and Ben Barker, who were working for Goodyear in Akron, Ohio. Pye invented a conveyor belt slitter that could take up to a ten-ton roll of belt and slit it to customer specifications, an innovation which was the spur both men had been seeking to form their own company. Setting up shop in Atlanta, the partners made a deal with their former employers to cut, slit and distribute Goodyear's belts, thus launching an industrial supply company, in 1936, which today serves more than eight hundred customers from its Forest Park headquarters and Savannah branch location. In 1951 they moved to a new warehouse at the corner of Pryor and Garnett in Atlanta. It's all gone now, town down to build a MARTA station, but at the time it had been the site of the original Ford dealership in the city.

From those humble beginnings years ago, Pye-Barker Engineered Solutions has emerged as a major provider of engineering services, as well as representing top tier industrial equipment manufacturers. It sells, fabricates, packages, services, repairs and installs all the equipment it represents, and backed by its team of dedicated professionals, has garnered a well-earned reputation for integrity, expertise, and customer service. In its early years, the fledgling company experienced steady growth, supplying belts to a series of high-profile clients, such as Georgia Power, U.S. Steel Birmingham, Georgia Marble, and others. With Pye serving as president and Barker handling the sales force, the business boomed, in no small part due to the vision of its founders, who were quick to add prestigious suppliers to their list, including 3M, Rust-Oleum, Falkand Rexnord, among others. Many of those early vendors are still around today, illustrating Pye-Barker's commitment to nurturing long standing relationships with its clients and customers.

SHARING THE HERITAGE

With Ike Scott as his sales manager, Lindsey grew the company in the direction he foresaw as most profitable, towards larger-ticket, engineered items. Conveyor belts were starting to be less profitable, so Lindsey ("Hub"), started the Hydro-Air Engineering division, giving customers a comprehensive pump and compressor service. Henceforth, Pye-Barker would sell, maintain and fix this equipment in-house or in the field, as necessary. Hydro-Air proved to be very profitable, and a group of both old and new faces joined the division in the late 1960s and the early 1970s. John Lunsford, Ed McDonald, Bill Spencer, Leroy Childers and others steered the company in the direction that Hub had envisioned. This included a 1968 agreement in which Pye-Barker Engineered Solutions became the Georgia distributor for Viking Pump, Inc. Pye-Barker has proudly represented Viking, who since 1911 has been an industry leader in the world of positive displacement gear pumps, for over fifty years.

In 1974, Pye-Barker's headquarters was moved to its present location in Forest Park, Georgia. Today, Pye-Barker's main focus is on pumps, compressors, blowers and vacuums, engineered solutions, parts and repairs. Pye-Barker prides itself in its total commitment to product quality; product knowledge and applications; inventory; and professionalism. This commitment is underscored by the company's policy of holding a $1.5 million+ inventory in its warehouses, ready to be "picked and packed" for immediate response to its clients' needs. Further, its close relationships with manufacturers,

After this auspicious start, the company was poised for transition, as Pye handed over the reins to the next generation of leadership, naming another Georgia Tech engineer, W.H. "Hub" Lindsey, president.

Manufacturing Success in Georgia

and its extensive network of partners, assures that crucial deadlines are met. Company President Eric Lunsford notes that currently its three main lines are Viking Pump and Gardner Denver air compressors and Gardner Denver blowers, and that Pye-Barker is continually working to add more engineering services to its offerings, as well as increasing its service capabilities and expanding its geographic footprint.

Since its inception, a big part of Pye-Barker's success has been its insistence on asking the right questions, of itself and of its customers. It takes the time to understand the unique challenges of its customers' businesses. "Are your pumps too big or too small?" "Are they located correctly?" "Were there problems with the original design?" By posing these, and other basic questions, and following through on them, Pye-Barker has been able to successfully forestall and correct innumerable "performance killing mistakes" for its clients over the years. That is why the company's first step with every client is a Design Needs Assessment. The company boasts that 94.3% of service calls are resolved on the first visit. This is evidence of Pye-Barker's commitment to unmatched customer service, and exemplifies the long-standing company legacy of dedication to hard work and the old-school way of doing business it has practiced every day since opening its doors back in 1936.

The need for greater online interaction with customers, team members, and partners in the early 2020s inspired Pye-Barker to initiate their new online Tech Training in which participants share their experiences. The company sees this as an ongoing investment to provide online background information for customers and valued partners by providing a library of on-demand information they can access anywhere. Pye-Barker also offers live masterclasses, overview styled webinars, and online training to provide customers with the background they need to make facilities operate efficiently and minimize down time.

To learn more about Pye-Barker and its history, products, services, and online resources, please visit www.pyebarker.com.

American Metalcraft Inc.

Founded in 1986, American Metalcraft Inc. is a leader in the architectural aluminum metal manufacturing market with experience and a diverse project portfolio. Gary Gotfredson, a structural engineer, founded American Metalcraft as a small fabrication shop off Howell Mill Road in Atlanta. Slowly, the shop and the size and breadth of AMI's projects grew in capabilities, employees and national presence. Gary saw a need in the metal market for PVDF (polyvinylidene difluoride) coatings and founded a second company in 2004, Finishing Dynamics in Villa Rica. By 2010, the two companies merged offering engineering, custom fabrication, and finishing under one roof, saving its customers base time and money. AMI works with material installers, roofers, glass and glazing companies, general contractors, curtain wall contractors, and more, to create solutions that "balance the aesthetic vision for a project with the right materials and products."

AMI creates products for both exterior and interior applications, rain screen and metal panel systems, custom sunshades, infill, perforated and shadow box panels, brake metal, column covers, and ornamental metal. Examples of American Metalcraft's work are part of its corporate headquarters, other office buildings, health facilities, schools, airports, government facilities, parking structures, bridges and more. With more than three decades of experience and innovation, AMI now boasts a coast-to-coast presence with projects ranging from the LG Headquarters in Englewood, New Jersey, the National Marine Corps Museum in Quantico, Virginia, Fort Bliss Hospital in El Paso, Texas, the Research Center at the University of Idaho, and the Fourteenth Street Bridge in Atlanta, Georgia.

In 2017, Holly Gotfredson, daughter-in-law of the company founder, purchased American Metalcraft, Inc. Her background in art, marketing/advertising and manufacturing, provides "a unique perspective in merging the aesthetic goals for a project with the nuts and bolts of bringing it to fruition." Holly takes pride in maintaining the highest degree of quality, performance, and excellence that goes into each product. AMI has maintained an active presence in its community partnering with the Carroll County Humane Society, the Veterans Empowerment Organization, the S.H.A.R.E. House of Douglasville, and the Backpack Program for the Carroll County School System. Holly participates in professional and industry outreach, through speaking and interacting in a variety of programs and professional panels. In 2018, AMI received its certification as a 100% Woman-Owned Small Business, and in 2019, Holly was recognized as one of Metal Forming and Fabrication Magazine's "Women of Excellence" honorees. This year Blue Print Magazine featured her in their "Women in Construction" series. Recently, AMI developed two AIA approved classes for continuing education credits. The company now has fifty-four employees in three states, new projects, an expanded sales effort through a larger manufacturing rep network, and is positioned for a future of growth and success. For more information visit AMI at: americanmetalcraft.com or (770) 459-3605.

Manufacturing Success in Georgia

KaMin Performance Minerals

Operating at the intersection of nature and technology, KaMin Performance Minerals is a leading supplier of fine and ultra-fine kaolin clay. Initially developed for paper filler applications, advances in technology over the years have enabled expansion into diverse markets such as packaging, health and beauty, construction, rubber, polymer, coatings and inks. Founded in 1926 as Twiggs Huber, Inc., the company began as a small local operation, working with the ceramic and paper industries. After a fire destroyed the original plant, the J.M. Huber family bought out Twiggs-Huber, Inc., and the company became part of the J.M. Huber Corporation. With its strategic location along the kaolin-rich Georgia fall line, the J.M. Huber Clay Division began to thrive and grow establishing its reputation as a leading innovator. In 1973, the company became the first in the industry to produce ultra-fine, high-brightness kaolin. Following its sale to IMin Partners in 2008, J.M. Huber Clay Division became KaMin. Four years later, KaMin became the global leader in fine particle kaolin clay, acquiring the Brazilian kaolin company, CADAM. Headquartered in Macon, KaMin's largest operations are in Georgia, with mine and benefaction plants in Macon, Sandersville, and Wrens. Its sister facility in Brazil and logistics operation in Belgium underscore KaMin's ability to serve the market worldwide. From its modest beginnings more than ninety years ago, KaMin is today listed in the top one hundred export companies in the United States by the *Journal of Commerce* (JOC) serving customers in more than sixty countries across five continents. KaMin's $4.5 billion impact to Georgia's economy is significant, as both an employer and a major contributor. The company's passion for kaolin clay drives KaMin's customer-focused innovation and excellence. The company's immense reserves of premium fine and ultra-fine kaolin in both Georgia and Brazil set it apart from all other producers. The company pioneered unique processing methods and applications expertise for fine particle technology. Their fine particle clays are the most widely used worldwide in numerous coating applications. KaMin's clays are currently used in hundreds of different formulations in dozens of industries, and its brands have set the industry standard in numerous applications. KaMin is continuously awarded for its corporate stewardship. It has received the Georgia Mining Association's Good Neighbor Presidents Award for twenty consecutive years. It has been active in supporting Earth Day, and has worked with the Ocmulgee Water Trail Partnership, the Beta Club, the Twiggs County Partnership, Mercer University and Homes of Hope. Proud of its heritage of providing "value from the ground up," KaMin is ready for the future, focusing on its goal of becoming the global leader in performance minerals that enables innovative product solutions for daily life. To learn more about KaMin and its products and services, visit kaminsolutions.com.

SHARING THE HERITAGE

DeNyse Sign

Jennifer and Allen DeNyse started making signs in the basement of their Douglasville, Georgia home in 1983. From this small start, the dynamic duo built a multi-million-dollar architectural sign business in a bustling 105,000 square foot manufacturing facility. When asked about their company philosophy, this family centered business responds, "We believe in keeping our commitments, good communication, and delivering quality products." Since inception, DeNyse Companies has developed a specialized skillset and diverse product offering. They are a full-service company, providing design, fabrication, installation, service and repair for architectural signage, commercial signage, lighting, and solar products.

During the early years, DeNyse focused primarily on marketing and manufacturing signage for the residential industry, starting out as Woodgraphics. The purchase of a small commercial sign shop in 1985 opened the door to explosive growth in the commercial sign industry. As the product offering continued to grow through acquisition, Woodgraphics became DeNyse Companies. DeNyse Companies is now one of the largest sign manufacturing companies in the Southeast led now by second generation Mark DeNyse. Certifications and awards have enhanced the DeNyse reputation. In 2001, DeNyse Companies successfully completed the rigorous process to become a Woman-Owned Business and currently holds certifications with The Women's Business Enterprise National Council (WBENC), the National Women Business Owners Corporation (NWBOC), and the City of Atlanta.

Numerous DeNyse projects have received awards from organizations such as the United States Sign Council (USSC) and Signs of the Times. DeNyse has also been named one of Atlanta's Best Places to Work by *Atlanta Magazine* and was ranked on Inc. 5000's as a fastest growing company for 2020. While DeNyse provides services nationwide, they are always proud of the local projects such as College Football Hall of Fame, The World of Coca-Cola,

Manufacturing Success in Georgia

SunTrust Park and the rebrand to Truist Park, home of the Atlanta Braves, as well as the rebrand of the historic Equitable Building to Georgia's Own that includes largest LED signage in the South East, which adds to Atlanta's unique skyline.

DeNyse Companies is also dedicated to giving back to the community through support on both an executive and individual level. They believe that true success is achieved through a responsible, well-rounded business practice that includes community outreach. DeNyse Cares, a charity organization started by employees, is dedicated to providing donations and volunteer time to many community programs.

DeNyse Companies' team of over 155 employees proudly offers nationwide award-winning services, including design, fabrication, installation, and maintenance of commercial signage and architectural elements. Employees often express that the DeNyse Company is "Overall a very creative and exciting place to work," "I love what I do and enjoy the people I work with." Based on the needs of customers, DeNyse has the vision to take them to the next level-visually. For more, visit denyseco.com.

SHARING THE HERITAGE

135

WORKS CITED

"7 Reasons Why Chicken Reigns King in Georgia." *Atlanta Magazine.* January 27, 2018. Accessed 4 February 2020.

"About the Plant." *Kia.* Accessed 29 February 2020.

Altamaha Riverkeeper. Accessed 21 April 2020.

"Barbary Wars, 1801-1805 and 1815-1816." United States Department of State. Office of the Historian. Accessed 19 December 2019.

Bauer, Olivia. "Lack of Broadband Access Holds Back Rural Georgia." 16 May 2020. Accessed 8 June 2020.

Beasley, John P. "Peanuts." *New Georgia Encyclopedia.* 08 April 2019. Accessed 04 February 2020.

Bellury, Phillip. "Gulfstream Aerospace Corporation." 19 August 2013. "Maule Air." 19 August 2013. *New Georgia Encyclopedia.* Accessed 28 May 2020.

Berry, Diana Ramey. "Cultivating Race: The Expansion of Slavery in Georgia, 1750–1860." *Journal of American History*, vol. 99, no. 4, Mar. 2013, pp. 1234–1235.

Bluestein, Greg. "GM to Hire 1,000 at New Atlanta IT Center." *Atlanta Journal-Consitution.* January 10, 2013. Accessed 29 February 2020.

Bowers, Paige. "Cagle's." *New Georgia Encyclopedia.* 31 July 2018. Accessed 04 February 2020.

Bowers, Paige. "Royal Crown Cola Company." *New Georgia Encyclopedia.* 19 August 2013. Accessed 22 January 2020.

Brooks, Rebecca Beatrice. "Construction of the USS Constitution." History of Massachusetts Blog, 30 July 2018. Accessed 18 December 2019.

Burse, Sabrina. "Contributing to the Defense of Our Nation: Houston County Leaders Announce Plans for Software Engineering Facility." *13WMAZ.* 06 March 2020. Accessed 11 June 2020.

"Cannon's Point Preserve." *Golden Isles Georgia.* Accessed 19 December 2019.

Carabello, Joanna S. "College of Management at Georgia Institute of Technology." *New Georgia Encyclopedia.* 19 June 2019. Feb. 02 June 2020. *Club Car.* Accessed 29 February 2020.

Cooksey, Elizabeth B. "Crawford County." 31 October 2018. "Treutlen County." 25 October 2018. *New Georgia Encyclopedia.* Accessed 28 January 2020.

Cooksey, Elizabeth B. Accessed 26 May 2020.

Davies, Lisa. "The Augusta National Golf Club: A Brief History." *Street Directory.* Accessed 29 February 2020.

Deaton, Thomas M. "Beaulieu of America." 07 June 2018. "J & J Industries." "World Carpets." 24 May 2013. 19 August 2013. *New Georgia Encyclopedia.* Accessed 11 December 2019.

ComSouth. Accessed 7 June 2020.

Delta Tech Ops. Accessed 30 May 2020.

Drake, Taylor. "Robins Air Force Base Unveils New Communications System." *13WMAZ.* 12 June 2020. Accessed 13 June 2020.

Edwards, Marla, and John D. Toon. "Georgia Institute of Technology (Georgia Tech)." *New Georgia Encyclopedia.* 30 August 2018. Accessed 02 June 2020.

E-Z Go. Accessed February 29, 2020.

Fair, John D. "Henry Tift (1841-1922)." *New Georgia Encyclopedia.* 19 August 2013. Accessed 10 December 2019.

Firestone, David. "Mill Town Mourns its Mill, then Reinvents itself." New York Times, 21 January 2002. Accessed 10 December 2020.

Fleming, Molly, "Diet Coke Sales Overtake Classic Coke as the Soft Drinks Giant Navigates the Sugar Tax [in Great Britain]." *Marketing Week.* July 16, 2018. Accessed 24 January 2020.

"Forest Industry Continues to Boost Georgia Economy." *All On Georgia.* 18 December 2019. Accessed 31 July 2020.

Frank, Andrew K. "Mary Musgrove (ca. 1700-ca. 1763)." *New Georgia Encyclopedia.* 05 October 2019. Accessed 13 December 2019.

"Georgia's Approach to Rural Broadband." Georgia Technology Authority. Accessed 9 June 2020.

Georgia Forestry Association. Accessed 18 December 2019.

"Georgia Grown Pecans." Georgia Department of Agriculture. Accessed 5 February 2020.

"Georgia Highway 316: Georgia's Innovation Corridor." Gwinnet Chamber of Commerce: *Georgia Innovation Corridor Joint Development Authority.* Accessed 10 June 2020.

"Georgia's High-Tech Corridor: U.S. Highway 341." Georgia General Assembly 02 HR 1327/AP. Accessed 13 June 2020.

Georgia Info: Galileo. Accessed 5 February 2020.

Georgia Manufacturing Alliance. Accessed 15 January 2020.

Georgia State Historic Markers. Accessed 9 December 2019.

Giebelhaus, August W. "Coca-Cola Company." *New Georgia Encyclopedia.* 06 June 2017. Accessed 9 December 2019.

Gordon, John Steele. "King Cotton." *American Heritage*, vol. 43, no. 5, Sept. 1992, p. 18. Accessed 15 December 2019.

Griffin, Joy. "Georgia-Pacific." *New Georgia Encyclopedia*. 19 August 2013. Accessed 17 April 2020.

Guide to the Robins Region Georgia. Robins Regional Chamber. St. Simons Island, Georgia: 365 Degree Total Marketing, 2017.

Haire, Brad. "Hurricane Michael Changed Georgia's Pecan Industry." *Farm Progress*. October 17, 2018. Accessed 19 December 2019.

Hall, Anna. "Lover's Oak Loses Branch After Being Hit by Truck." *The Brunswick [Georgia] News*, 13 October 2019. Accessed 19 December 2019.

Hamburger, John. "Chik-fil-A Reports Record Revenue in 2019, Profits Up by 54.2 Percent." *Franchise Times: The News Source for Franchising*. April 2020. Accessed 17 July 2020.

Hammond, Sarah. "Robins Air Force Base to Integrate Drones in Everyday Operations." *13WMAZ*. 22 January 2020. Accessed 11 June 2020.

"'He was Real Friendly:' 1941 Berry high school grad recalls meeting Henry Ford." *Marietta Daily Journal*. September 25, 2014. Accessed 27 February 2020.

"History of the Georgia Forestry Commission." *Georgia Forestry Commission*. Accessed 18 December 2019.

Hudson, Paul S. "Ben Epps (1888-1937)." *New Georgia Encyclopedia*. 13 July 2018. Accessed 28 May 2020.

International Paper. Accessed 19 April 2020. Jackson, Ed and Charles Pou. "This Day in Georgia History: October 26." *GeorgiaInfo*. The University of Georgia. Accessed 25 May 2020.

Jackson, Edwin L. "James Oglethorpe (1696-1785)." *New Georgia Encyclopedia*. 01 August 2019. 13 December 2019.

Jones, Barry W. "Pecans." *New Georgia Encyclopedia*. 30 November 2018. 4 February 2020.

Jones, Tyler H. "Brunswick Auto Port Double Capacity in 2017." *The Brunswick News*. 20 October 2017. Accessed 29 February 2020.

Kelso, Alicia. "Chick-Fil-A's Growth Trajectory Fueled by Demand for Simplicity." *Forbes*. Accessed 2 February 2020.

Kingsford Charcoal. History. Accessed 27 February 2020.

Kiss, Sr., Stephen. "On TV Westerns of the 1950s and '60s." New York Public Library. 1 December 2012. Accessed 7 March 2020.

"Land Lottery Records." *Georgia Archives*. Accessed 18 December 2019.

Lawrence, Richard Z. "Does Manufacturing Have the Largest Employment 'Multiplier' for the Domestic Economy?" for *Peterson Institute for International Economics*. 22 March 2017. Accessed 4 August 2020.

Lee, Maggie. "Payne City Officially Dissolved." *The Telegraph*, 1 April 2015. Accessed 27 January 2020.

Lummus. "History." Accessed January 27, 2020.

Marsh, Ben. "Colonial Immigration." *New Georgia Encyclopedia*. 9 May 2019. Accessed 2 March 2020.

"Martin-Marietta Aggregates." *Gray-Jones County Chamber*. Accessed 29 July 2020.

McDuffie, Justin. "Georgia's High-Tech Corridor: A Myth?" *13WMAZ*. 15 March 2017. Accessed 11 June 2020.

Morris, Michael. "The Peculiar Case of Mary Musgrove Matthews Bosomworth: Colonial Georgia's Forgotten Leader." *International Social Science Review*, vol. 71, no. 1/2, Jan. 1996, p. 14. EBSCOhost. Accessed 15 December 2019.

Morrison, Carlton A. *Running the River: Poleboats, Steamboats & Timber Rafts on the Altamaha, Ocmulgee, Oconee & Ohoopee*. Saltmarsh Press.

Mumm, Josie. "8 Fascinating Facts About the Busiest Airport in the World, which sees 107 Million Passengers a Year and Employs 63,000 People." *Business Insider*. 2 June 2019. Accessed 29 February 2020.

"My Ancestors Didn't Come Over on the *Mayflower*. They Were Just Standing There When It Docked." *Quote Investigator*. 11 March 2015. Accessed 4 March 2020.

"Nanotechnology in Georgia – Companies, Research, and Degree Programs." *Nanowork*. Accessed 12 June 2020.

National Oceanic and Atmospheric Administration Office of Ocean and Coastal Resource Management (NOAA) and Georgia Department of Natural Resources Coastal Resources Division. Georgia *Coastal Management Program: Environmental Impact Statement*, December 1997. Accessed 17 December 2019.

"Naval Stores." United States Department of the Interior. Moore's Creek National Battlefield. Site Bulletin. Currie, North Carolina. Accessed 19 December 2019.

Navicent Health. "Heart Center, featuring the Luce Heart Institute. Accessed 29 February 2020.

Niesse, Mark. "Georgia Unveils Plan for Internet Service in Rural Areas." *The Atlanta Journal-Constitution*. 29 May, 2019. Accessed 8 June 2020.

Newkirk, Margaret. *Online Athens: Athens Banner-Herald*. "Bill Gates Foiled by Georgia's Powerful

Vidalia Onion Regulators." 8 April 2019. Accessed 28 February 2020.

Patankar, Siddharth Vinayak. "Who is Kia? The 7 Things You Didn't Know About Kia Motors." 27 April 2017. Accessed 29 February 2020.

Patton, Randall L. "Carpet Industry." 05 October 2019, "Interface, Inc.." 19 August 2013. "Shaw Industries." 24 May 2013. "Chenille Bedspreads." 5 October 2019. Accessed 06 March 2020.

Pilgrim's: A Global Story. Accessed 3 February 2020.

Press Release Tift Cotton Mill: The Georgia Museum of Agriculture & Historic Village.

Pritchett, Amy R. "Hartsfield-Jackson Atlanta International Airport." *New Georgia Encyclopedia.* 19 June 2017. Accessed 30 May 2020.

"Real value doesn't come from a supplier. It comes from a partner." *WestRock.* Accessed 25 May 2020.

Reed, Germaine M. "Charles Herty (1867-1938)." *New Georgia Encyclopedia.* 17 September 2019. Accessed 11 December 2019.

Reynolds, Jacob. "Global Hawk Drone Arrives at Robins for the First Time Ever." *13WMAZ.* 24 May, 2017. Accessed 13 June 2020.

"Richter Produce Announces Historic Merger; Welcomes Generation Farms." *Richter Farms,* 6 Apr. 2016. Accessed 27 February 2020.

Robichaud, Kathleen. "Georgia Research Alliance." *New Georgia Encyclopedia.* 22 May 2013. Web. 02 June 2020.

Sanders, Sigrid. "Providence Canyon." *New Georgia Encyclopedia.* 26 July 2017. Accessed 22 May 2020.

Sands, Patrick. *Kia Motors Celebrates Decade of Manufacturing in Georgia.* 18 November 2019. *Kia Motors Produces Three Millionth Vehicle in the U.S.* 15 September 2019. Accessed 29 February 2020.

Savannah Economic Development Authority. "Port of Savannah: A Window to the World." Accessed 29 February 2020.

"Savannah History." *Visit Historic Savannah.* Accessed 17 December 2019.

"Scholfield's Iron Works." *The Atlanta Constitution.* 16 May 1880.

Scott, Thomas A. "Lockheed Martin." *New Georgia Encyclopedia.* 10 December 2019. Accessed 28 May 2020.

SoftWear. Accessed 7 June 2020.

Sullivan, Buddy. "Naval Stores Industry." *New Georgia Encyclopedia.* 08 June 2017. Accessed 03 March 2020.

Sweet, Julie Anne. "Bearing Feathers of the Eagle: Tomochichi's Trip to England." *Georgia Historical Quarterly,* vol. 86, no. 3, Fall 2002, p. 339. Accessed 15 December 2019.

"The Birth of the Navy of the United States." *Naval History and Heritage Command.* Accessed 18 December 2019.

"The History of Sea Island Cotton." *Welcome to Beaufort, South Carolina.* Accessed 19 December 2019.

The JEFFERSON MILLS, INC. v. UNITED STATES of America. [1965]259 F. Supp. 305 (1965) Civ. A. No. 1029. (United States District Court N. D. Georgia, Gainesville Division.).

Toon, John D. "Entomopter Artificial Insect." *New Georgia Encyclopedia.* 23 July 2018. Accessed 28 May 2020.

United States Marine Band. "The Marine Hymn." Accessed 19 December 2019.

"USDA Invests $5 Million in Broadband for Rural Georgia Communities." United States Department of Agriculture Press. 21 February 2020. Accessed 8 June 2020.

Varnum, Ashley. "Automotive." *Georgia Industries.* Accessed February 29, 2020.

Vidalia Onions. "What Makes a Vidalia Onion?" Accessed 28 February 2020.

Vintage Gun Leather. "Bona Allen Company History." Accessed 7 March 2020.

Weinberg, Carl. "Poultry." *New Georgia Encyclopedia.* 31 July 2019. Accessed 22 January 2020.

"What is Nanotechnology?" *National Nanotechnology Institute.* Accessed 12 June 2020.

"Who We Are." *Graphic Packaging International.* Accessed 19 April 2020.

Wickersham, Mary Eleanor, and Robert P. Yehl. "The Cotton Mill Village Turned City: A Retrospective Analysis of Three of Georgia's Smallest Cities." *Journal of Urban History,* vol. 40, no. 5, Sept. 2014, pp. 917–932. Accessed 14 January 2020.

Wilcox, Dianne Dent. "Along the Garrison Road." *The Jones County News.* 16 July 1992. *Planes, Trains & Heroes: A Story of Warner Robins and the Robins Region.* Warner Robins Convention & Visitors Bureau and HPN Books, San Antonio: 2019.

Williams, Arden. "Bibb Manufacturing Company." *New Georgia Encyclopedia.* 16 September 2019. Accessed 14 January 2020.

Williams, Jayne. "GALILEO." *New Georgia Encyclopedia.* 26 May 2015. Accessed 01 June 2020.

Willis, Kiersten. "The Comfort for Frontline Heroes Campaign Benefits Workers on the Front Line of the Coronavirus Pandemic." *Atlanta Journal-Constitution.* 4 April 2020. Accessed 5 August 2020.

Woods, Robert O. "A Turn of the Crank Started the Civil War." *Mechanical Engineering,* vol. 131, no. 9, Sept. 2009, pp. 54–56. SEP-5. Accessed 17 December 2019.

Zainaldin, Jamil S. "Charles Lindbergh in Georgia," "Delta Air Lines," "Eastern Air Lines," ""Museum of Aviation." *New Georgia Encyclopedia.* Accessed 30 May 2020.